Deliciously Italian

Deliciously Italian

From Sunday Supper to Special Occasions,
101 Recipes to Share and Enjoy

F<small>EDERICO AND</small> S<small>TEPHEN</small> M<small>ORAMARCO</small>

CITADEL PRESS
Kensington Publishing Corp.
www.kensingtonbooks.com

CITADEL PRESS BOOKS are published by

Kensington Publishing Corp.
850 Third Avenue
New York, NY 10022

All Kensington titles, imprints, and distributed lines are available at special quantity discounts for bulk purchases for sales promotions, premiums, fund-raising, educational, or institutional use. Special book excerpts or customized printings can also be created to fit specific needs. For details, write or phone the office of the Kensington special sales manager: Kensington Publishing Corp., 850 Third Avenue, New York, NY 10022, attn: Special Sales Department; phone 1-800-221-2647.

Illustrations by Patricia Peacock-Evans

CITADEL PRESS and the Citadel logo are Reg. U.S. Pat. & TM Off.

First printing: October 2006

10 9 8 7 6 5 4 3 2 1

Printed in the United States of America

Library of Congress Control Number: 2006926716

ISBN 0-8065-2787-0

For Samuel Alonzo Moramarco,
the newest addition to the family!

Contents

Introduction

IN THE NEIGHBORHOOD in Brooklyn where I grew up, my friend Ralph's father owned a popular local restaurant called Pugliese's. "Mr. Ralph," as we called him, was obsessed with having "the best" of everything. He used the best ingredients for the food he served, dressed elegantly in the best clothes, and always drove a Cadillac because, as he said, in his thick Italian accent, "It's-a da best!"

We followed Mr. Ralph's principle throughout this book, selecting only the best and discarding anything that fell short of perfection. We searched and sampled, asked and interviewed, and dug into our family's past and our ancestors' heritage to come up with these recipes.

In addition, we've contacted the best Italian chefs throughout the country at the best Italian restaurants, and they've graciously sent us their best recipes. From Little Italy in Providence, Rhode Island, to the splendid Italian eateries in San Francisco's North Beach, we've gathered these "best of the best" to supplement recipes that have been handed down from one generation to the next.

But recipes are only as good as the ingredients in them, and an absolute requirement for excellent Italian food is always to use the freshest ingredients available. You'll hear this throughout our book: the most important factor in

Italian cooking is the freshness of the ingredients. And there's no better way to ensure that freshness than to grow many of the important ingredients yourself. Ingredients such as tomatoes, basil, and parsley are hearty plants and easy to grow in just about any environment. You don't need to be a master gardener to grow them. If you absolutely can't grow your own, you might think about shopping, at least for produce, in a local farmer's market, if you're lucky enough to have one in your community.

What follows, is a selection of recipes—the food grandma used to make as well as the food on the menus of today's most successful Italian restaurants—that will make dinner a special event at your home. In short, we think these recipes are terrific and hope you do too.

—*Federico Moramarco*

WHEN MY FATHER approached me about doing a sequel to *Italian Pride*—this time a cookbook—my first reaction was to blanch. "But Pop, I'm *not* a cook!" I exclaimed. Now, you're probably thinking this admission isn't the best way to start a book of 101 recipes, but let me clarify: I said I am "not" a cook, not that I "can't" cook. In fact, I think that almost anyone *can* cook, with a little diligence and patience.

And that's exactly what I learned from embarking on this project. After a year of talking to, and collecting recipes from, Italian restaurants and families, each with their own stories and recipe advice; working with my father (who has been a gourmet chef for as long as I can remember) on holidays and weekends, hosting cooking and tasting parties with my friends, getting their valuable input on these recipes; and cooking and experimenting on my own, immersing myself in the rich culture of Italian food, I can now proudly exclaim "I *am* a cook!"

We hope those of you who feel as I did will walk away from this book emboldened with a new confidence and a new skill. Seasoned chefs will also find challenges, as we have included recipes at every level. And we hope everyone will discover at least one new dish to share with family and friends.

Discover your "inner chef," learn a little about Italian culture, and, most important of all, have fun making a great meal!

—Steve Moramarco

Deliciously Italian

The Italian Kitchen

The kitchen is the center of the Italian home. In traditional Italian families, Mama and Papa would often take turns at the stove and the familiar and comforting smell of bubbling tomato sauce permeated the entire house. On Sundays or holidays, the kitchen was always abuzz with activity as relatives and guests created and sampled rich, flavorful meals.

But the Italian kitchen is a practical place as well, and it needs to be properly equipped if you want to create the delectable flavors described on these pages. Here is a brief overview of the essential tools and other items you will need to make most of these recipes successfully.

Essential Ingredients for Your Cupboard, Fridge, or Freezer

TOMATO SAUCE

Depending on how adventurous you are in the kitchen, you can keep fresh tomatoes and a large can each of whole tomatoes, crushed tomatoes, stewed tomatoes, diced tomatoes, pureed tomatoes, or tomato paste, each of which goes through various steps to become a homemade tomato sauce. If you must, you can even keep several jars of pre-made, store-bought tomato sauce for emergencies; the point is always to have some kind of tomatoes on hand as, odds are, the recipe will call for some.

Homemade tomato sauce also stores well in the freezer—just place it in tightly closed plastic containers and freeze for up to three months.

GARLIC

Garlic is an essential ingredient in many Italian recipes. While some recoil from its powerful odor, it nonetheless contains vitamins A, B, and C, which help bolster the immune system. Garlic is grown and sold as bulbs that are covered by a paperlike skin and should feel firm to the touch. You can store garlic in the cupboard or fridge for at least a month, so buy a few at a time— you're going to need them.

OLIVE OIL

This gorgeous green liquid is perhaps the lifeblood of Italian cooking. The best of the best is the one they call *extra virgine* or extra virgin, which means it contains the juice from the first cold pressing of the olive. Most recipes in this book call for extra virgin, but if you cannot find or afford this kind, a good-quality, regular olive oil will do. But be aware that olive oils vary greatly in quality, and a serious Italian cook never skimps on this ingredient. You can get information about recent harvests of premium olive oils throughout Italy at www.olio2go.com.

PARMESAN CHEESE

In Italy, this sharp and pungent cheese is called Parmigiano-Reggiano, which refers to the region where it originated eight hundred years ago and where it is still made today. It is the topping of choice for many pasta sauces and a fine flavoring for just about any dish. You can buy it pre-grated, but it is best when bought in a hard chunk from the cheese shop and freshly grated atop the warm meal. Other topping options are Pecorino Romano (a rival topping made from ewe's milk); Grana Padano, a similar hard, gratable cheese from Lombardy that some prefer on pizza; or Ricotta Salata, a dry version of ricotta, popular in Sicily, sprinkled over pasta. Whichever you choose, you should always have some grated cheese of this type on hand.

HERBS AND SPICES

Fresh basil, fresh Italian parsley (the flat-leaved kind), and oregano (either dried or fresh) are indispensable ingredients in any Italian kitchen. When it comes to basil and parsley, you can never have too much—so it's always good to have fresh on hand. They're easy to grow in season, even in a windowsill herb planter. Oregano is the only Italian herb that's often preferable in its dried state rather than fresh. In Italian markets you can buy oregano dried on the stem, but keep it in a tightly sealed container. Dried red pepper flakes are also good to have on hand when you want to spice up a dish a bit, and fresh rosemary is always useful to have around as well.

Essential Kitchen Tools

WOODEN SPOON

If there is one item the Italian kitchen cannot do without, it's a simple spoon made of wood. It's perfect for mixing risottos, tasting sauces, and whacking the back of the hand of kitchen intruders.

GOOD SHARP KNIVES

Many if not all the recipes call for something to be cut, sliced, cubed, or julienned. A good chef's knife—eight or ten inches, depending on what you feel most comfortable with—is the perfect tool. But more important than the size is that you keep it sharpened. Dull knives are like dull people—not very useful in the kitchen. An investment in a good knife sharpener will repay itself in culinary satisfaction many times over. You should also have a boning knife, a slicing knife, a paring knife, and a serrated knife of some sort to slice bread.

MEAT MALLET

Often, meat or chicken fillets need to be flattened out or pounded into shape, as does beef or veal for cutlets or a braciole (rolled beef). This instrument comes in both metal and wood, and is essentially a weight on a stick that helps with a wide range of tasks in the kitchen. It will also help release any pent-up aggressions you have instead of releasing them on your guests. If you do not have a meat mallet, a rolling pin or the flat side of a meat cleaver will do in a pinch.

PIZZA STONE AND PIZZA PEAL

You simply cannot make a thin-crust pizza (see p. 221) without these items. A regular oven will normally not get hot enough, but with a circular pizza stone, you will be able to get the crust to crispy perfection. A peal is akin to a large wooden spatula and is the device you use to transfer your raw pizza from countertop to oven without a terrible mess or burned fingers. It can also be used as a serving tray once you take the pizza out of the oven.

PASTA MACHINE

If you want to have a truly *homemade* pasta dinner, you need to have a pasta machine. But the simple, hand-cranked type is actually preferable to the fancier, hard-to-clean electronic types. For any serious Italian cook, it's a must-have in the kitchen, and a decent one costs under $50.

FOOD MILL

Well, this is really not an *essential* tool, but it is very helpful, especially if you make your own tomato sauce. A food mill separates the skin and seeds from the juice and core of the tomato and gives the sauce exactly the right texture—neither too chunky nor too watery.

SOME OTHER TOOLS YOU MAY WANT TO HAVE ON HAND

Garlic press, pizza cutter, ravioli cutter, metal spatula, basting brush, fat separator, zester, baking pan, Dutch oven, measuring cup, and measuring spoons.

ADDITIONAL FOOD ITEMS

Bread crumbs (both seasoned and plain), eggs, flour, sugar, vanilla bean, saffron, white truffles, and truffle oil. Actually, the list is endless, but as you Italianize your kitchen, you'll settle on the things you need to have most.

Some Basic Italian Cooking Terms You Should Know

Most of the recipes are written as simply as possible, but there are a couple of words with which you may not be familiar.

Al dente: You will see this term in virtually every pasta dish in this book. It literally means "to the tooth," and signifies when the pasta is at its chewy perfection. Many American chefs have a tendency to overcook pasta so that when the sauce is added it turns into mush. You can check to see if pasta is ready the old-school way, by throwing a strand against the wall—if it sticks, the pasta is ready. Or if you don't like the idea of streaks of pasta on your walls, just bite into a strand or two until you find the consistency that suits you.

Julienne: No, it's not the name of a beautiful woman, it's merely a fancy way of saying "cut into thin strips." And although it's a French word, we include it here in our Italian cookbook because of its ubiquity in the cooking parlance.

Reduce: This is a way of "boiling off" creams or sauces to a lesser amount (e.g., reduce by half). It is an inexact measurement, just use your eyes and make sure you don't burn your pan.

Deglaze: When meat is cooked in a skillet or baked in the oven, the recipe often calls for the pan to be deglazed. This simply means adding some liquid, usually wine, to the pan to help scrape up the tasty little brown morsels that remain. It's a good idea to remove the pan from the heat, especially when using wine so that the pan doesn't catch fire.

Marinara: Literally means "mariner's style" and may have something to do with the fast tomato sauce the wives of fishermen made to serve with the catch of the day. But today it refers to virtually any tomato sauce that is made without meat—with only tomatoes, herbs, and spices.

Ragù: A meat sauce, also sometimes known as Bolognese, typical of the sauce made in Bologna. It usually includes some vegetables, such as carrots, onions, or celery, or all three and a little cream.

Dolce: Pronounced "*dol*-che," meaning sweet, but more generally used as a generic term for desserts of any kind.

A Note on the Cookbook

In writing and assembling this book, we have attempted to create clear, concise recipes, primarily for beginning and intermediate chefs. To aid you in this process, we included some helpful information in the heading.

First, "Serving Size" will let you know how many mouths you can feed with each particular dish. Most recipes in this book were designed for a serving of four, but there are many exceptions. If you want to make more (or less), adjust your measurements accordingly. Don't worry too much about "exact" measurements. After a very short time, you should be able to estimate tablespoons, cups, half cups, and so on. Italian cooks rarely measure things out. In fact, one well-known Italian chef has published a cookbook with no measurements at all—only ingredients and directions.

"Preparation Time" includes the time it takes both to prepare and cook your dish. Of course, depending on your expertise in the kitchen, these numbers may be wildly off the mark. Use them as a rough guide—don't set your stopwatch to them.

We have also included a "Difficulty" level for each recipe. This is a number from 1 to 5, with a "1" given to items that have few ingredients, require little or no cooking, and can be prepared quickly. From there, as ingredients, cooking skill, and preparation time increase, so does the difficulty level.

And while most Italian cookbooks arrange their recipes according to a traditional Italian meal—*antipasto* (appetizer), *primi* (first course, usually pasta or rice), *secondi* (meat or fish), *contorni* (side dish), *insalate* (salad), and *dolce* (dessert)—we decided it might be more useful to American cooks to subdivide the categories, including a special vegetarian section (see p. 203). After all, most Americans (and even Italian Americans) rarely eat a six-course meal.

In the back of the book, we've created special menus (see appendix A) with courses that complement one another, along with a wine suggestion, courtesy of Chef Aldo Blasi of San Francisco's esteemed Ristorante Milano and Luca Vannini of Zigzagando Wines. Please, feel free to experiment. A recipe is really just a guide to a dish that was made successfully in this fashion; it is not carved in stone. These recipes do come from chefs and families who have honed their methods and ingredients for years, but once you get the hang of it, try adding your own special twist for fun and flavor.

Finally—take your time to read the recipe carefully and completely before you begin cooking. As Grandfather Stephen Moramarco (Federico's father) used to say, "Chi va piano va sano e va lontano" (Who goes slowly goes in good health and travels far).

Buon' Appetito!

Antipasto

Antipasto literally means "before the meal," and Italians usually like to nibble on something before digging into the first course of dinner. Antipasti (the plural form) can be hot or cold, cooked or raw, elaborate or simple. There are often several kinds of antipasto that precede the meal, antipasto a piedi (antipasto served while guests are still standing) and antipasto a tavola (antipasto served at the table). In Sicily, antipasti are called grape 'u pitittu, *which in the Sicilian dialect means "mouth openers," and that is, of course, what they are intended to do. Look over our selection of delectable mouth openers, and soon you should be able to begin designing your own.*

Tomatoes with Basil, Olive Oil, and Mozzarella

The tomato is a staple ingredient in most Italian food. Coupled with basil, a little olive oil, and some fresh mozzarella, this appetizer is a good, quick way to jump-start the palate before a hearty meal. The recipe is simplicity itself, but as always, is only as good as the quality and freshness of the ingredients. This dish is best with *pomodori* plucked fresh from the vine. There are many ways to serve this dish, but we found these arrangements most satisfying and striking in their presentation.

MAKES: *4 servings* • PREPARATION TIME: *10 minutes* • DIFFICULTY: *1*

2 whole, vine-ripened heirloom or yellow tomatoes (or one of
  each), cut crossways in ¼-inch slices
12 large whole (not dried) basil leaves
½ pound fresh whole milk mozzarella, cut into ¼-inch slices
Salt and freshly ground pepper
3 tablespoons (about) extra-virgin olive oil, preferably unfiltered
Sprig of basil for garnish

Place sliced tomatoes around the edge of a dish in a circle, slightly overlapping. On top of each slice, place a fresh large basil leaf, nearly covering each tomato piece in its entirety. Next, top each leaf with a generous slice of mozzarella. When dish is assembled, season to taste with salt and pepper and drizzle olive oil over the layers. Garnish center of the dish with the basil sprig. Serve immediately.

VARIATION: Use a small basket of red or yellow pear tomatoes (or both), cube the mozzarella instead of slicing it, chop the basil leaves instead of using them whole, and toss together in a bowl with olive oil. Sprinkle with salt and pepper to taste, and toss again.

2.

Federico and Stephen's "Instant" Antipasto Misto

These days, with so many delicious imported Italian snack items available in ready-to-serve jars or cans, it's easy to create your own signature antipasto in minutes, just like a major Italian restaurant. This is our version, made mostly with ingredients we have on hand in the cupboard or the fridge.

It's simple to make many variations of this dish, but remember—antipasti should be quick to make and appealing to the eyes. Other items that work well in this mix are sliced tomatoes, asparagus spears, mozzarella or provolone cheese, green olives, marinated baby onions, and capicola (spicy Italian ham) or salami. This is really less a recipe than it is an assemblage, so assemble away!

MAKES: *4 servings* • PREPARATION TIME: *15 minutes* • DIFFICULTY: *1*

4 slices prosciutto
4 slices mortadella
4 slices rosemary ham
4 slices Asiago cheese.
4 slices Italian fontina cheese

4 slices tallegio cheese
¾ cup black Sicilian cured olives or pitted Kalamata olives
¾ cup marinated mushrooms with garlic
1 red or yellow bell pepper, sliced in strips
3 celery stalks, cut in 2" sticks
Parsley for garnish

On a large oval platter, alternate slices of the cold cuts and cheese around the edges. In the center, mound olives, mushrooms, and peppers in separate spaces. Separate center from meats and cheese with celery sticks. Garnish with parsley sprigs and serve with a basket of fresh crisp Italian bread slices.

3.

Stuffed Artichokes
Carciofi Ripieni

The artichoke is one of the oldest foods known to humans—dating back to Italy and Sicily in the fourth century BC. The artichoke's tender, chewy heart is actually the flower's bud, which is a brilliant purple when in bloom. The artichoke was also thought to enhance sexual prowess among males—an ancient Sicilian Viagra, if you will. While we can't guarantee anything, we're sure that this recipe will stimulate at least your appetite. If you're feeling adventurous, you can add 2 or 3 anchovy filets to the breadcrumb mix.

MAKES: *4 servings* • PREPARATION TIME: *2 hours, 15 minutes* • DIFFICULTY: *3*

1 cup store-bought Italian-seasoned bread crumbs
¼ cup water
¼ cup extra virgin olive oil
¼ cup Pecorino Romano cheese
¼ cup chopped parsley, very finely chopped
3 cloves garlic, very finely chopped
Salt and pepper

4 medium-sized artichokes
1 cup water
½ lemon

Thoroughly mix the bread crumbs, water, oil, cheese, parsley, garlic, salt and pepper to taste. The mixture should be damp, but not soggy. If it doesn't feel damp, add some water a bit at a time until you have the desired consistency.

Remove the tough exterior leaves from the artichokes and discard. Squeeze juice of the lemon half into the cup of water. Dip the remaining artichoke in lemon water for just a few seconds. Then, with a serrated knife, cut across the top portion of the artichoke and discard top. Cut the bottom stem off as well. Split open vertically and clean out the interior fibrous chokes. Stuff the middle with bread crumb mixture.

Once all the artichokes have been filled, place in a 9 x 13-inch baking pan and add water covering to about half the standing artichokes. Drizzle olive oil on the stuffed vegetables and into the water. Cover and bring to a boil using two burners if necessary. Then lower heat on each burner and simmer covered over very low heat for about 1½ to 2 hours.

Check periodically to be sure that water remains at midlevel. Add additional water if necessary. Remove from water, place on serving tray, and eat leaves together with stuffing, either at hot or at room temperature. All parts of the artichoke, by this time, should be soft and edible. While the inner leaves can be eaten whole, the outer leaves are enjoyed by biting into them and pulling them off the artichoke meat, discarding the leaf husk.

4.

Stuffed Zucchini

Zucchini Ripieni

Monica's Trattoria first opened its doors in March 1995, occupying a small storefront in Boston's North End. The four brothers of the Mendoza family offered a simple menu of hot and cold sandwiches, delicious homemade pastas, and grilled meats and seafood. As news of this eatery spread by word of mouth, the tiny space was constantly crowded with hungry customers.

This recipe for stuffed zucchini is one of their trademark dishes, and it transforms a simple zucchini into a very satisfying appetizer.

MAKES: *4 servings* • PREPARATION TIME: *1 hour* • DIFFICULTY: *2*

Preheat oven to 350 degrees.

2 medium-sized zucchini
½ red onion
½ carrot
½ red bell pepper
1 egg
½ cup of cream

3 basil leaves, chopped
Salt and pepper
½ cup grated Parmesan cheese
Pinch of chopped parsley

Cut zucchini in half lengthwise. Scoop out the inside of the zucchini and dice it, setting the shell aside for baking. Dice the onion, carrot, and bell pepper.

In a bowl, whisk the egg and cream; then add the vegetables and stir in basil and salt and pepper to taste until well combined.

Place the vegetable mixture back into the zucchini shells, and sprinkle with Parmesan and parsley. Finally, put the stuffed zucchini onto a baking sheet lightly coated with oil, and bake for 25–30 minutes. Serve warm.

5.
Caponatina alla Siciliana

As Sicilian food becomes more mainstream, many people are discovering dishes that have long been traditions on the island but never crossed over to the mainland. This is one of those appetizers that, on tasting it, people exclaim, "Why didn't somebody tell me about this before?" Sometimes referred to as *caponata*, this dish contains several staples of the Sicilian diet: eggplant, capers, and olives. This particular version comes to us from the Di Fiore family, who, at a recent reunion, had compiled the family recipes and distributed a cookbook to all attendees.

MAKES: *4 servings* • PREPARATION TIME: *1 hour* • DIFFICULTY: *3*

½ cup plus 2 tablespoons olive oil
2 cups diced celery
6 cups diced, peeled eggplant
Salt
1 minced small onion
⅓ cup wine vinegar

2 tablespoons tomato paste diluted in 1 cup water
1 tablespoon sugar
1 tablespoon chopped parsley (optional)
1 large green olive
1 tablespoon capers
Salt and pepper

Heat ½ cup of the olive oil in a skillet over medium heat and sauté celery for seven minutes, stirring occasionally. While celery is cooking, salt eggplant to reduce bitterness.

Remove celery from the pan with a slotted spoon and set aside.

Add eggplant to oil in same skillet and sauté for 10 minutes, stirring often. Remove eggplant and drain on plate with paper towels.

Put 2 tablespoons of the oil (if necessary) into the same skillet and sauté until soft, but don't let the onions turn brown. Dilute tomato paste in 1 cup water. Add vinegar, sugar, and diluted tomato paste. Reduce heat, cover and simmer for 15 minutes. Add eggplant, celery, optional parsley, olives, capers, salt and pepper to taste. Cover and simmer for ten more minutes. Serve with a basket of crisp Italian bread.

6.

Bruschetta or Crostini

Bruschetta (pronounced *broos*-keh-ta) literally refers to a bare slice of toasted bread, which is rubbed with garlic and drizzled with olive oil. *Crostini* are small pieces of toast, usually garnished with chopped tomatoes, pesto sauce, mushrooms, or any of dozens of other possibilities. These days, the terms are used somewhat interchangeably. We like to make a bruschetta first, then top it with something just before serving. Here's a delicious way to do that.

MAKES: *4 servings* • PREPARATION TIME: *10-15 minutes* • DIFFICULTY: *1*

Preheat oven to 375 degrees.

FOR THE BRUSCHETTA:
1 French white (not sourdough) baguette, cut into ⅓-inch slices
½ cup garlic-infused olive oil

FOR THE CROSTINI:
2 cloves garlic, peeled (optional)
4 Roma tomatoes, chopped in small pieces

½ cup chopped basil leaves
½ cup extra virgin olive oil
Additions for crostini:
shredded mozzarella cheese, sliced mushrooms, sliced Kalamata
    olives, or olive paste (also known as *olivata*).

To prepare the bruschetta: Preheat the oven to 375 degrees. Drizzle bread slices with garlic olive oil (or rub slices with optional garlic and drizzle olive oil over them) and place in single layer on a large baking sheet.

Toast slices until slightly brown; turn over and brown the other side. This process shouldn't take more than five minutes. Be careful not to burn the bruschetta.

To prepare the crostini: Mix tomatoes with basil leaves in medium bowl and toss with garlic olive oil until well blended. Place a spoonful of tomato mixture on each bruschetta; return to oven for one minute and serve.

VARIATION: If you're using any of the additions, sprinkle on top before reheating. Olive paste can be spread on some of the slices and served alone.

7.
Rice Croquettes
Arancini di Riso

Arancini means "little oranges," and that's what these plump (and very filling) rice croquettes look like when they're done. They are great fun to make—you can do it for, or with, a crowd, as they are very literally a hands-on project. Originally a Sicilian dish, it has spread in popularity throughout the Continent. This is a version from Apulia, located at the heel of the Italian boot.

MAKES: *about 8 large rice cakes* • PREPARATION TIME: *45 minutes* • DIFFICULTY: *2*

    2 12-ounce cans chicken broth
    4 cups water, boiling
    1 pound arborio rice (2 cups)
    2 large eggs
    2 tablespoons minced fresh parsley
    ½ cup shredded Parmesan cheese
    Salt and freshly ground pepper
    ¼ pound mozzarella cheese, cut into ¾-inch cubes

1 cup store-bought Italian-seasoned bread crumbs
2 cups vegetable oil

Pour the chicken broth into 4 cups boiling water in a medium saucepan. Place the rice in a large saucepan over medium heat and slowly add the diluted broth a cup at a time, stirring constantly with wooden spoon until liquid is absorbed after each addition and rice is al dente (cooked but firm). Drain and cool.

Add eggs, parsley, Parmesan cheese, and salt and pepper to taste to rice and mix thoroughly. With both hands, as if you were packing a snowball, form the rice mixture into balls the size of a small orange.

Insert mozzarella cube into the center of each ball and reshape. Roll balls in seasoned bread crumbs to coat the surface. Heat the vegetable oil in a medium saucepan until tiny bubbles form. Deep fry the rice balls, turning on all sides two or three at a time, until golden brown. Drain on paper towels.

8.

Roasted Peppers with Cheese
Pepperoni Arrostiti con Formaggio

Established in 1984, Trattoria Contadina is owned and operated by the Correnti family. Serving dinners to a mix of San Francisco locals and tourists, the Trattoria is noted for its hearty portions as well as its excellent food. This appetizer is one of the signature antipasto dishes that combines several Italian cheeses with bell peppers. Take note: this is a very hefty appetizer. Serve only with a light meal, like Chauncey Street Frittata (see p. 205) or Spinach and Apple Salad (see p. 49) because you won't have room in your tummy for much else after this.

MAKES: *4 servings* • PREPARATION TIME: *30 minutes* • DIFFICULTY: *2*

    4 whole red or yellow bell peppers
    8 ounces cold bel paese cheese, shredded (see note 1, p. 28)
    8 ounces Asiago cheese, shredded
    4 cups shredded mozzarella cheese
    1 cup marinara sauce (see note 2, p. 28)

> 1 cup heavy cream
> Pinch of red pepper flakes

Roast whole bell peppers (see note 3 below). Cut each pepper in half length-wise and clean out seeds and membranes. Mix bel paese and Asiago cheese together and stuff peppers with cheese mixture. Top off each pepper half with a fist of shredded mozzarella.

In a large saucepan or skillet, mix marinara and cream and place the stuffed peppers one at a time, stuffed sides up, into sauce. Add a pinch of red pepper flakes for added flavor. Simmer covered until cheeses are melted. Serve hot, with additional sauce on the side.

NOTES:

1. Bel paese cheese is available at most markets or substitute Italian fontina, if you can't find it.

2. You can use prepared sauces widely available in supermarkets or tomato sauce on p. 77 and add cream to it.

3. *To roast peppers:* Roast peppers whole in pan under an oven broiler or threaded on a long skewer and held over a gas flame on stovetop or grill. Roast to blacken skin. Using electric or gas, turn occasionally to blacken all sides. Remove from heat source and place peppers in a brown paper bag to

sweat for 5 to 10 minutes. Remove from bag and rub off blackened skin. Do not run under water.

9.

Prosciutto-Wrapped Shrimp

Janie Losli and Ken Cassinelli, the co-owners of Apertivo Restaurant in San Diego, California, share this easy and tasty delight. Apertivo specializes in what they call Italian Tapas, bite-sized portions of Italian foods, served with wine. Patrons can enjoy a wide variety of dishes for a reasonable price, and one of the most popular is their prosciutto-wrapped shrimp. It sounds so simple, yet the combination of meat and shellfish is not common in Italian appetizers. The "secret" to this recipe is simply picking the best shrimp and prosciutto available from your local market. Once you have those, the rest is easy, but it's sure to impress guests or family.

MAKES: *4–6 servings* • PREPARATION TIME: *10 minutes* • DIFFICULTY: *1*

20 large or extra large, precooked, deveined shrimp
10 thin slices prosciutto, cut vertically in half
3 tablespoons extra virgin olive oil
Lemon wedges for garnish
Parsley, chopped for garnish

Wrap the shrimp in 1 x 6-inch strips of prosciutto and secure them with wooden toothpicks.

In a small sauté pan, heat the extra virgin olive oil until just below smoking.

Add the shrimp, but don't overcrowd the pan. Let them crisp on one side (about a minute) before turning and crisping on the other side.

The quicker you cook the shrimp the better because they get too tough when overcooked. Remember, the shrimp we recommend for this recipe are already precooked. When they are crisp on both sides, arrange on a plate, drizzle with more olive oil, and garnish with a lemon wedge and chopped parsley. Serve immediately.

10.
Panzanella

This dish originated as the quintessential peasant food, made in the poorest villages in southern Italy. During the long, hot summers, when nothing but stale bread, tomatoes, and basil were available to eat, mothers would stretch the food by making panzanella. This meal gave their families something nourishing, intensely flavored, and completely satisfying to put in their stomachs. Panzanella's peasant roots are long gone, however, as these days it's taught by chefs at the Culinary Institute of America and served in upscale restaurants. Now you can bring the tradition back around to the family by making and serving this version at home.

MAKES: *4 servings* • PREPARATION TIME: *15 minutes* • DIFFICULTY: *1*

1 loaf dried Italian bread (at least 2 days old)
½ cup plus 2 tablespoons olive oil
1 tablespoon unsalted butter
4 garlic cloves, peeled and minced

5 medium fresh tomatoes (preferably homegrown) chopped into
 1-inch cubes.
¼ cup high-quality balsamic vinegar
2 cups basil, leaves sliced into ¼-inch slices
Salt and pepper

Preheat the oven to 350 degrees. Cut bread into small (½-inch) cubes and bake in oven for 6 or 7 minutes until browned.

Heat 2 tablespoons olive oil and butter in a large skillet over medium-low heat until butter melts. Add garlic and stir fry for about a minute. DO NOT LET GARLIC BURN. Add bread cubes to skillet and mix with garlic.

In a large bowl, toss the bread cubes, tomato cubes, and basil. Add salt and pepper to taste and let sit for a few minutes until the flavors blend. Serve in individual pasta bowls.

11.

Artichoke Hearts with Crabmeat
Couri di Carcofi con Granchio

Antonino Germano opened the La Scala Restaurant in Baltimore's historic Little Italy in 1995; its cozy environs and personal service help create a romantic and welcoming table. The menu offers Italian cuisine from all regions of Italy, making it a great place to explore new dishes. This recipe is a regular menu item at La Scala and can be easily done at home using fresh or canned crabmeat (*not* imitation crabmeat) and marinated artichoke hearts in jars.

MAKES: *4 servings* • PREPARATION TIME: *15 minutes* • DIFFICULTY: *1*

4 ounces (about ¼ pound) jumbo lump crabmeat
6 whole marinated artichoke hearts, halved
2 tablespoons capers
1 tablespoon olive oil
½ cup white wine
½ lemon
Salt and pepper

Heat olive oil in medium skillet over medium heat and sauté crab, artichokes, and capers for 5–6 minutes. Add white wine and continue to sauté for another two minutes. Reduce heat, and squeeze lemon over crab mixture in pan. Heat for another minute and remove. Add salt and pepper to taste and serve immediately with fresh bread.

12.

Fried Smelt

A popular tradition among many Italian Catholics on Christmas Eve revolves around a meal called The Feast of the Seven Fishes. Not only is the number seven significant in Catholicism (the Seven Sacraments, the Seven Days of Creation), but eating fish was also considered a form of penitence before Christmas Day communion.

Robert Tinelli, whose family is from Calabria, had many a memorable Christmas feast growing up in an Italian enclave in West Virginia. "In our family, it wouldn't be Christmas without smelt," says Robert, referring to these tasty, almost bite-sized little fish, which are inexpensive and available frozen in many stores. Cooking smelt can be fun for kids too, because you shake a bag filled with flour to coat the smelt for frying.

MAKES: *6–8 servings* • PREPARATION TIME: *15 minutes* • DIFFICULTY: *2*

2–3 pounds smelt, frozen, heads removed
1 cup all-purpose flour
Salt and pepper

2 eggs
1 cup milk
¼ cup olive oil
2 garlic cloves, minced
Pinch of red pepper flakes

Wash the smelt and pat dry. Place flour seasoned with some salt and pepper for taste into a paper bag. Whisk eggs and milk together in a shallow bowl. Dip smelt in egg mixture, drop them into the bag, and shake until all the fish are well coated with the flour.

Heat olive oil in a cast iron skillet (or regular frying pan) and add the garlic and red pepper flakes. If the oil sizzles when you add a drop of water, then add the fish in batches to the heated oil until brown and crispy on each side. Don't crowd the fish in the pan. They cook quickly.

Remove fish from pan with a slotted spoon and let drain on paper towels. Repeat until all the smelt is done, adding more oil if necessary. Line a serving platter with a fresh paper towel and transfer smelt to that dish. Sprinkle generously with salt and pepper. Then eat 'em whole!

13.

Parmesan Chips
Frico

This interesting appetizer is one of those rare exceptions where domestic pre-grated Parmesan cheese is preferred to the "real" Parmigiano-Reggiano cheese (see "The Italian Kitchen," p. 3). The imported cheese is actually too dry for this recipe, says Piero Selvaggio, owner of Valentino, one of Los Angeles' finest Italian eateries for over three decades. You can serve these chips alone as an *assaggino* or *antipasto a piedi*—the little morsel you offer guests when they arrive. Or you can use the frico as a container, for example, to hold the Prosciutto-Wrapped Shrimp (see p. 30).

MAKES: *4 servings* • PREPARATION TIME: *½ hour* • DIFFICULTY: *2*

Special equipment: Rolling pin or base of cup (to form basket)
2 cups pre-grated, domestic Parmesan cheese

Buy a tub of already grated Parmesan cheese and process it in a food processor until it has a powdery consistency. Heat a nonstick skillet over medium heat.

(Any higher and the oil in the Parmesan cheese comes out, and makes a gummy texture.)

Sprinkle enough Parmesan cheese to cover just the bottom of the pan (for a 9-inch pan, use about 3–4 tablespoons of cheese). When it is golden brown—which can take less than 1 minute—use a pair of tongs to grab the edge and gently lift it out of the pan. Turn and cook the other side briefly. Blot excess oil on a paper towel. Working quickly, shape the frico (chip) on a rolling pin to form a cylinder or around the base of a cup to form a basket. Serve alone or as just suggested.

14.

Capuzi Garbi

This fantastically flavorful appetizer is a collision of flavors (including beer!) that will send your taste buds reeling. It comes from Bruno Viscovi, owner and chef of Albona Ristorante Istriano located in San Francisco, California. Bruno prides himself on his family's Istrian roots. Istria is located in Croatia on the Adriatic coast, but across from Trieste.

Albona Ristorante is the first and only Istrian restaurant on the West Coast, and while this is not strictly an Italian recipe, we decided to include it because Bruno is so passionate about food, and his menu is truly unique, with influences from the Italians, Austrians, Hungarians, Slavs, Spaniards, French, Jews, Greeks, and Turks that have populated the area. This recipe has flavors from all of them at once!

MAKES: *6–8 servings* • PREPARATION TIME: *1 hour* • DIFFICULTY: *3*

    1 32-ounce jar sauerkraut, rinsed and drained
    3 tablespoons peanut oil
    2 slices prosciutto fat, diced

1 tablespoon butter
1 onion, finely chopped
1 Pippin or Granny Smith apple, peeled and cut into ¼-inch slices
2 slices prosciutto, finely diced
1 bay leaf
4 whole cloves
Pinch crushed red pepper
6 ounces beer
2 tablespoons chopped parsley
1 pound sausage (optional, see note 1, p. 42)

Heat the oven to 225 degrees.

Drain the sauerkraut and squeeze out as much of the liquid as possible. Put the oil in a large nonreactive skillet (see note 2, p. 43) at very low heat, and add the prosciutto fat and let it render, without scorching, for 10 minutes.

Discard the scraps of fat and add the butter. Sauté the onion to a golden brown at medium heat. Add apple slices and sauté for two minutes. Add the diced prosciutto, laurel leaf, cloves, pepper, and stir for 1 more minute.

Turn the heat to high and add the sauerkraut a little at a time, stirring constantly until the liquid has evaporated. Deglaze (p. 7) with 3 ounces of the beer. Reduce the heat to very low, cover the skillet, and simmer for 25 minutes.

To prevent scorching, stir occasionally and add the remainder of the beer as needed. When all the liquid has been absorbed, transfer the uncovered skillet to the warm oven for 15 minutes. Discard bay leaf, and mix in the parsley before serving.

NOTES:

1. Any type of sausage would enhance this recipe. Lightly brown the sausage in a separate ovenproof skillet. Incorporate it into the mixture just before the mixture begins to simmer. After you remove the skillet from the oven, remove the sausage and slice it into ¼-inch slices. Place the slices at the side of the plate on which you have placed the sauerkraut. Serve with ½ teaspoon of European-style mustard.

2. A nonreactive skillet has an interior that will not adversely affect foods, such as stainless steel, anodized aluminum, enamel linings, and nonstick surfaces (although some of these may have temperature limitations for oven use).

Salads

INSALATE

In Italy and throughout most of Europe, salads are rarely served before the main course, but rather after it, as a kind of palate cleanser. In Italian homes, salads are made with whatever greens happen to be in season, with various additions from the Italian cupboard. We have included a few distinctive salad types, but the general rule is to find some greens you like, add a little oil and vinegar along with some herbs —oregano, basil, or parsley—toss with salt and pepper, and serve. Croutons, nuts, dried fruit, or tomatoes and other additives make the salad a little more substantial.

15.

Blood Orange and Onion Salad

The deep red color of the blood orange, combined with the purple and the green of red onions, rosemary, and chicory, makes this a particularly colorful dish. And unlike other Italian salads, this salad is usually served as a first course, as a kind of vegetarian antipasto.

The blood orange was originally introduced into Sicily by the Arabs, sometime between the ninth and tenth centuries. Its juicy red insides and tart flavor distinguish it from a traditional orange and are clearly the inspiration for its romantic name. The rich Sicilian soil and sun allowed these oranges to flourish in the region, and the blood orange has become a signature Sicilian ingredient and a symbol of Sicilian passion.

MAKES: *4 servings* • PREPARATION TIME: *15 minutes* • DIFFICULTY: *1*

2 blood oranges
2 medium red onions
1 bunch of chicory

FOR THE DRESSING:
4 tablespoons extra virgin olive oil
1 tablespoon lemon juice
2 tablespoons fresh rosemary, chopped finely
Salt and pepper
Rosemary sprigs to garnish

Peel oranges and slice thinly, removing any seeds. Slice red onions in ¼-inch slices. Spread chicory over a large platter and arrange slices atop it, alternating oranges and onions.

To prepare the dressing: Mix olive oil, lemon juice, and rosemary in a small bowl, season with salt and pepper, and pour over salad. Garnish with rosemary sprigs.

16.

Operatic Spring Greens with Gorgonzola, Walnuts, Currants, and Three-Cheese Dressing

This salad is so called because we made it one evening in the Spring before going with friends to see Rossini's comic masterpiece *The Barber of Seville*. It's lively, dramatic, and intense, as most opera is, and the wide range of flavors is very satisfying. Add some sliced chicken breasts and it becomes a meal in itself.

MAKES: *4 servings* • PREPARATION TIME: *15 minutes* • DIFFICULTY: *1*

FOR THE SALAD:
1 8-oz. package mixed Spring Greens (or mix your own combi-
    nation)
½ cup crumbled Gorgonzola cheese
½ cup chopped walnuts
½ cup dried currants (or dried cranberries)

FOR THE DRESSING:
4–5 teaspoons balsamic vinegar
½ cup high quality extra-virgin olive oil
2 tablespoons grated Parmigiano-Reggiano cheese
2 tablespoons grated Asiago vecchio (aged Asiago, not the fresh
    kind)
2 tablespoons grated Romano cheese

Mix salad ingredients together in a large bowl. Mix all dressing ingredients in a small jar or bowl until emulsified. Pour half the dressing over the salad and toss vigorously. (Operatically!) Serve salad on four individual salad plates, and pour the remainder of the dressing into a serving bowl and pass separately, stirring before adding to salads.

17.

Spinach and Apple Salad

This recipe comes to us from San Francisco's Venticello Ristorante, located atop historic Nob Hill. It's a popular spot for lovers and tourists, who enjoy both the view and the sound of the clanging trolley that glides on by. An intriguing combination of sweet apples, crunchy pine nuts, sharp cheese, and leafy spinach greens gives this salad its special "bite." A sweet-and-sour honey/balsamic vinaigrette dressing tops it off.

MAKES: *4 servings* • PREPARATION TIME: *10 minutes* • DIFFICULTY: *1*

Preheat oven to 375 degrees.

8 cups fresh baby spinach
2 apples (your favorite variety)
½ cup pine nuts
¼ cup pecorino cheese (grated)

FOR THE VINAIGRETTE:
½ cup balsamic vinegar
½ cup honey

Rinse spinach and let drain for 5 minutes. Wash and core apples; then cut in half.

Spread pine nuts on a small baking pan. Toast pine nuts in oven for 5–6 minutes. (Be careful not to let them burn.)

To prepare vinaigrette: Combine honey and vinegar in a bowl and mix until they are blended.

Slice all the apples into a half moon shape. In a bowl, combine spinach, toasted pine nuts, and vinaigrette. Mix well. Place salad mixture on 4 plates; place half of sliced apple atop each one. Sprinkle with pecorino cheese and serve.

18.

Italian Pride Salad

This is our invention: an easy, colorful salad that foregrounds the colors of the Italian flag: red, white, and green. (Okay, the gorgonzola cheese adds a little blue as well—that's for Italian American pride.) There are dozens of variations you can make for this one and many ways to dress it, but if you want it to reflect Italian Pride, keep things red, white, and green.

MAKES: *4 servings* • PREPARATION TIME: *10 minutes* • DIFFICULTY: *1*

Special equipment: screw-top jar

FOR THE SALAD:
1 head butter lettuce, ripped in pieces
1 large head radicchio, shredded
2 Roma tomatoes, sliced diagonally
4 ounces gorgonzola cheese, crumbled

FOR THE DRESSING:
1 cup extra virgin olive oil
⅓ cup red wine vinegar
1 clove garlic, minced
2 tablespoons lemon juice
1 teaspoon sugar
½ teaspoon dry mustard
½ teaspoon dry oregano
1 teaspoon chopped basil
Salt and freshly ground pepper

To prepare the salad: Toss lettuce and radicchio together. Add tomato slices and toss again. Sprinkle with gorgonzola cheese and any additional optional toppings (see variations).

To make the dressing: Combine all ingredients in a jar. Shake well to blend. Store in refrigerator until ready to serve. Right before serving, add ¼ cup dressing and toss again. Serve additional dressing alongside.

VARIATIONS: Add dried cranberries, pine nuts, slivered almonds, and croutons, whatever you like.

Soups

MINESTRA

If you're not having pasta, risotto, or polenta as a first course of an Italian meal, then you're probably having soup, which substitutes for those standards, especially in the winter. There are several classic Italian soups—Italian Wedding Soup, Minestrone, and Stracciatella—that are quite distinctive, and knowing how to make them will mark you as a true aficionado of "la cocina Italiana." Almost anyone can toss together a salad or boil pasta, but making a delicious soup requires both patience and skill and often separates serious cooks from dilettantes.

19.

Italian Wedding Soup

Although it's widely believed this soup is served at Italian weddings, it actually has nothing whatsoever to do with nuptials of any kind. The name of the soup comes from a mistranslation of the Italian *minestra maritata* (a "married" soup), referring to how well the ingredients—greens, meat, broth, and cheese—go together. Nonetheless, it's a classic Italian dish and makes a great starter or a hearty and satisfying meal in itself.

MAKES: *4 servings* • PREPARATION TIME: *2 hours* • DIFFICULTY: *3*

FOR THE MEATBALLS:
¾ cup Italian-seasoned bread crumbs
¾ pound premium lean ground beef
1 egg
Salt and pepper

FOR THE SOUP:
⅓ cup extra virgin olive oil
¾ cup onions, sliced
1 tablespoon garlic, minced
2 32-ounce containers of free-range chicken broth (or 4
    14.5-ounce cans plus 2 cups water)
½ cup zucchini, chopped in small pieces
¾ cup carrots, diced
¾ cup celery, diced
¾ pound escarole (or spinach), chopped
1 cup orzo
4 tablespoons grated Parmesan cheese
Salt and pepper
Pinch of nutmeg

To prepare the meatballs: Mix seasoned bread crumbs and ground beef in a large bowl. Add egg and mix all ingredients together. Season with salt and pepper to taste. Form into small (¾ inch or less) balls by wetting your hands and rolling the meat in your palms. Let dry on platter until ready to add to soup.

To prepare the soup: Heat the olive oil over medium heat in a large pot. Add onions and sauté until they are translucent. Add the garlic and continue to sauté, about five minutes longer. Add the chicken broth and bring to a boil over high heat. Add the zucchini, carrots, celery, and escarole, lower heat, and simmer for about 1½ hours or more or until vegetables are soft. Add meatballs, escarole, and orzo, and simmer for 10–15 minutes longer. Add cheese, stir, and season with salt, pepper, and nutmeg. Serve immediately. (The soup also keeps very well in the refrigerator for several days and tastes even better when served a second time.)

NOTE:

You can add an elegant touch to this soup by serving it in ovenproof bowls, topping each serving with a half cup of shredded mozzarella and melting and browning the mozzarella under the broiler for about 5 minutes before serving.

20.

Piedmont Autumn Soup

Here is a soup that is perfect for the crisp days of late autumn, when the leaves have changed color and the first whiffs of winter are in the air. The chicken livers give it an extra tang and the *tagliatelle* (a flat strip pasta) makes it a substantial and hearty dish. It requires a few different steps, but it is well worth the time and effort. This recipe comes from the Piedmont region of Italy where Guiliana Clerico created it, who, along with her husband Domenico, is one of Piedmont's outstanding wine producers.

MAKES: *6 servings* • PREPARATION TIME: *3 hours* • DIFFICULTY: *4*

1 4-pound chicken, cut in half
2 celery stalks, cut into thirds
1 carrot, cut into thirds
1 onion, peeled and quartered
10 assorted peppercorns
4 sprigs parsley
2 sprigs thyme

1 bay leaf
1 tablespoon extra virgin olive oil
Liver from the chicken, diced
2 sprigs fresh basil
2 sprigs fresh parsley
1 plum tomato, seeded and chopped
⅓ pound tagliatelle, broken into 2- to 3-inch pieces
Parsley and basil leaves for garnish
Salt and pepper

Place the chicken, celery, carrot, onion, peppercorns, parsley, thyme, and bay leaf into a large soup pot and add 3 quarts of water. Bring to a boil; then lower heat to simmer and cook for 2½ hours, skimming fat off the top every half hour or so. Remove the chicken and set aside. Strain the stock through a fine mesh strainer (for a thicker soup, press all ingredients through a food mill) discarding solids. Set soup pot aside. When chicken cools, remove skin and debone. Shred the dark meat, and refrigerate, and reserve white meat for another use.

Heat olive oil in small skillet and sauté the chicken livers for about 3 minutes. Return the strained stock to soup pot and bring to a boil; then lower heat once again to simmer. Add the basil and parsley sprigs, chopped tomato, and tagliatelle. Cook until the pasta is al dente (cooked but firm); then stir in the shredded dark meat chicken and livers. Discard bay leaf. Season with salt and pepper to taste. Serve in individual bowls garnished with basil and parsley leaves.

21.

Minestrone

You might say that minestrone is "soup for the Italian soul." Full of vegetables, beans and pasta, it combines the heartiest of Italian staple foods in one glorious and hearty broth. Eat it when you are sick and you will feel well; eat it while healthy and feel even better. Chef Giacomo Dresseno, co-owner of Primavera Restaurant in Ft. Lauderdale, Florida, is from Lake Como in northern Italy. The beautiful mountainous lake region, about an hour's train ride from Milan, is balmy in the summer but can get quite cold in the winter. Giacomo's minestone soup is just the ticket to keep you warm. (For more information on Lake Como, see *Italian Pride*, Reason 37.*)

MAKES: *8 servings* • PREPARATION TIME: *1 hour* • DIFFICULTY: *2*

> ¼ cup olive oil
> 1 potato, peeled and cut into ½ inch cubes

---

*Federico Moramarco and Stephen Moramarco, *Italian Pride: 101 Reasons to Be Proud You're Italian* (New York: Citadel Press, 2000).

⅔ stalk of celery with the leaves removed

1 medium zucchini, peeled

1 medium yellow squash

Green beans, handful, ends trimmed

1 cup butternut squash or pumpkin, peeled with seeds removed

1 carrot

1 small onion

2 quarts vegetable broth (chicken or beef stock can be used if a
richer flavor is desired) (see appendix E)

1 garlic clove, peeled and chopped

Salt and black pepper

Dash of cayenne

½ cup of cooked beans (see note, p. 66) or beans from a 15-ounce
can, with juice (see note, p. 62)

½ cup Fresh Tomato Sauce (see p. 77) or 1 large ripe tomato, diced

½ box (8 ounces) of ditalini rigati (or other small, hollow noodles)

Parmesan cheese, grated

Heat oil in a stockpot over medium heat. Add well-washed and diced potato, celery, zucchini, yellow squash, green beans, butternut squash, or pumpkin, carrot, and onion. Let vegetables cook for 3 minutes, stirring a few times; then add the broth, garlic, salt, black pepper, cayenne, beans, and tomato sauce or tomato, and let simmer for at least an hour (up to 1½ hours) to make sure carrots are cooked. Adjust seasoning, add the ditalini to the soup, and continue cooking until pasta is done. Adjust seasoning to taste again, and serve with freshly grated Parmesan cheese.

NOTE:

Choose your favorite beans to give your minestrone an individual touch.

VARIATION: Try Passato Di Verdura: same preparation as minestrone, but instead of adding the ditalini, use a food processor or blender to reduce to a cream consistency. If desired a splash of heavy cream or butter (or both) will add a creamy feel to the soup.

22.
Stracciatella

Carbonara's restaurant on Avenida Del Mar in San Clemente, California, is consistently chosen as the best Italian restaurant in the area. Since it is equidistant between San Diego and Los Angeles, it's a great place to stop for lunch or dinner when en route between cities. Tony Carbonara has kindly contributed his recipe for *stracciatella*, an Italian version of what many Americans might think of as egg drop soup. Often this soup is made with small meatballs, like the Italian Wedding Soup (see p. 55), but Tony has developed a vegetarian version that his Orange County regulars love.

MAKES: *4 servings* • PREPARATION TIME: *15 minutes* • DIFFICULTY: *2*

4 cups vegetable broth
8 ounces frozen chopped spinach, thawed and squeezed dry
1 tablespoon minced garlic
1 tablespoon extra virgin olive oil
2 tablespoons butter
2 large eggs

Salt and pepper
Grated Parmesan cheese

Combine broth, spinach, garlic, oil, and butter in a large saucepan. Bring to a boil; then simmer for 5 minutes. In a separate bowl, whisk the eggs thoroughly. While soup is simmering, stir it in one fluid circular motion while slowly pouring in the eggs. Let stand for a few minutes, season with salt and pepper to taste, and serve. Pass the Parmesan separately.

23.

Red Garbanzo Broth

Here is unquestionably the oldest recipe in this book. It goes back to the ancient Etruscans and is still popular in central and southern Italy. It was written down in the fifteenth century, in what is considered the first modern cookery book, *The Art of Cooking* by the eminent maestro Martino of Como. Martino's cooking was already legendary in his time, and thanks to his friend Platina, these recipes were transcribed during the Renaissance and printed for posterity. Recently updated for modern palates, the book nevertheless is a gastronomic classic and a fascinating peek at the life and food of the early Italians.

MAKES: *6 servings* • PREPARATION TIME: *3 hours (beans soaked overnight)* • DIFFICULTY: *3*

    5 tablespoons extra virgin olive oil
    1 clove garlic, peeled
    ¼ pound smoked pancetta, diced
    1 pound dried garbanzo beans (chickpeas) (see note, p. 66)

1 large sprig rosemary
1 bunch sage
1 teaspoon whole black peppercorns (or more)
½ teaspoon ground cinnamon
½ cup finely chopped Italian parsley
Salt
½ pound spaghetti, broken into 3 pieces
Parmesan cheese, grated

Heat 3 of the tablespoons of the oil in a large pot; add the garlic and pancetta. When the garlic has begun to brown, add the reconstituted chickpeas, cook for a few minutes, and then add hot water to cover. Add rosemary, sage, peppercorns, and cinnamon. Cover and cook for 2 hours over very low heat until the chickpeas have become very tender. At this point, strain half of the chickpeas (returning the strained liquid back to the pot), and puree in a food processor; then return to the pot. Continue to cook for 5 minutes before adding the parsley. Season with salt to taste, add the remaining tablespoons of oil, and serve hot.

NOTE:

Wash beans well and soak overnight in cool water with a pinch of baking soda. Strain overnight and rinse.

VARIATION: For those who like a heartier soup, after adding parsley, add broken spaghetti pieces while the soup is still boiling, and continue to cook over low heat until the pasta is al dente (cooked but firm) stirring to be sure that it does not stick to the bottom of the pot. Then season with salt to taste, add the remaining oil, and pass Parmesan cheese when served.

24.

Pasta and Bean Soup
Zuppa di Pasta e Fagioli

The setting of Café on the Green is idyllic—especially if you're a golfer. It overlooks the beautiful Richter Park Golf Course in Danbury, Connecticut, and at night, the spotlights illuminating some of the greens and fairways turn them into a kind of fairyland haven. But the ambience is only part of the attraction. It's consistently ranked one of the top restaurants in the Connecticut-Westchester County area, and it has a wine list "to die for," as the saying goes. When we asked the chef for one of their signature recipes, he sent us this soup, which will be forever immortalized as *pasta fazool* in the Harry Warren ballad "That's Amore."

MAKES: *4 servings* • PREPARATION TIME: *35 minutes* • DIFFICULTY: *2*

    1 cup cooked tubetti or any small tube-shaped pasta
    2 tablespoons virgin olive oil
    1 garlic clove, sliced
    1 leaf basil, chopped
    9 ounces canned cannelliini beans, drained

4 cups chicken broth (see appendix E) or canned
½ cup marinara sauce or store-bought marinara sauce
1 tablespoon butter
2 pinches of salt and pepper

Cook tubetti for about 15–20 minutes until al dente (cooked but firm), strain out water and put aside.

Put oil, garlic, and basil in heavy pot on medium to high heat and cook for 2–4 minutes until sliced garlic is translucent. Add beans and cook for 1 minute. Add chicken broth, marinara, butter, and salt and pepper to taste. Cook for 5–8 minutes until soup is boiling. Add tubetti and stir for 1 minute. Serve immediately in bowls with hot hearty Italian bread alongside.

Pastas and Sauces

For most Americans, pasta is synonymous with Italian food. From Piedmont to Apulia and from Sicily to Venice, each region of Italy has its distinctive type of pasta, and even within regions there is a remarkable multiplicity. A true pasta aficionado will distinguish long, thin strands of pasta by the millimeter. The thinnest strands are capellini or fidelini; next up the ladder are capelli or spaghettini; add a millimeter or so and you have spaghetti. Flatten that spaghetti and it's linguine. Broaden the linguine and it becomes fettucini or tagliatelle. Widen it even further and it turns into pappardelle. Pasta comes in all shapes and sizes: it can be a thimble (ditalini), a little ear (orecchiette), a butterfly (farfalle), or a pen point (penne). Pasta can be stuffed (ravioli, tortellini, cannelloni), layered (lasagna), made into tubes (rigatoni, mostaccioli), or curled like a corkscrew (fusilli). Add to this diversity (and these types hardly scratch the surface) the wide range of sauces that you can serve with it and you have an almost infinite variety. In this section we offer just a few of those possibilities.

25.

Homemade Fresh Pasta

Very few people make fresh pasta at home these days, but it is an Italian tradition well worth keeping alive. Most of us have become so accustomed to buying pastas in the dry goods section of the supermarket, that a generation may not even be familiar with what fresh pasta tastes like. And that is unfortunate, because for most sauces and dishes, the difference is considerable.

Many older Italian Americans remember watching their mamas make several days' worth of pasta at a time in the kitchen, kneading and shaping the dough in a variety of ways. We hope to rekindle those memories and help reinvigorate the art of making pasta dough by showing you how to do it yourself.

Here's the simplest, most delicious fresh pasta you can make, and it only requires two ingredients: flour and eggs. The first time you attempt this, it may take a lot longer than half an hour, but with practice you'll be whipping it up in no time flat, and you may never use dried pasta again!

MAKES: *6 servings* • PREPARATION TIME: *30 minutes* • DIFFICULTY: *3*

Special equipment: hand-cranked pasta machine

3 cups all-purpose flour
4 eggs

Mound flour on a clean surface and make a large well in the center. Break the eggs into the well and beat lightly, gradually incorporating some flour from the sides of the well into the eggs. Continue this process until more and more of the flour is absorbed, and the flour becomes a dough. If the dough seems dry, add a half eggshell of water to the mixture.

At first, the dough may be sticky and hard to handle. Dust both your hands with flour and knead dough for about ten minutes until it becomes soft and pliable. When it is completely smooth and only slightly moist, roll it into a ball and cover with a damp towel.

Break an egg-sized piece off the dough, flatten it, and run it through the widest setting of the pasta machine, drawing it into a long, wide ribbon. Fold ribbon in half and run through the machine again. Repeat this process about 5 or 6 times until dough is very smooth. (Be sure to fold dough in half each time you run it through the machine.)

After the fifth or sixth time through the machine, lower the setting a notch and run it through the machine without folding. Keep reducing setting until pasta is as thin or thick as you want it. (We usually stop at the second-to-lowest setting.) For long-stranded pastas, add attachment for the type of pasta you

are making (fettucini, linguine, spaghetti, capellini, etc.) and run the pasta through the attachment. Hang on a rack or lay on a table to dry slightly before cooking. For ravioli (see p. 119) or lasagna (see p. 215), lay pasta on a large floured table in long 4- to 5-inch wide sheets. Fresh pasta cooks very quickly and needs only a few minutes in boiling water.

Substitute your own homemade fresh pasta for any of the recipes that follow in this section.

26.

Fresh Tomato Sauce

Like fresh pasta, there is just no substitute for the taste of a sauce made with fresh homegrown tomatoes. If you're lucky enough to have a little space for a garden and can grow your own tomatoes in the spring, this is the perfect recipe for you to refer to when harvest time comes around.

If you absolutely must use store-bought tomatoes, make sure they are vine ripened, and use Roma tomatoes mixed with cherry tomatoes, because they make the sweetest sauce.

MAKES: *5–6 cups of sauce* • PREPARATION TIME: *1 hour, 45 minutes* • DIFFICULTY: *2*

3 tablespoons extra virgin olive oil
2 garlic cloves, minced
3 pounds homegrown tomatoes, preferably Roma or large cherry
  tomatoes or both
2 large carrots, peeled and chopped
2 stalks celery, chopped
1 sweet onion, peeled and diced

1 cup basil leaves, chopped
½ cup parsley, chopped
½ cup red wine
2 bay leaves, whole
1 tablespoon sugar
Salt and pepper

Heat olive oil over medium heat in a large Dutch oven or large heavy saucepan. When oil is hot, add garlic and sauté for a minute or so; then add tomatoes, carrots, celery, onion, basil, and parsley. Simmer for 1 hour over low heat, turning gently from time to time.

When tomatoes are soft and mixture is semiliquid, pour in small batches through a food mill set over a large bowl or other pot. (If you don't have a food mill, you can blend mixture in a food processor, and then pour through a strainer.)

After mixture is strained, return to large pot, add wine, bay leaves, sugar, and salt and pepper to taste, and simmer for another half hour or so. Discard bay leaves. Divide into 4 or 5 1-cup containers and store in freezer until ready for use.

27.

Classic Bolognese Sauce

The Emilia-Romagna region of Italy is the great heartland of Italian food, and some of the greatest cooking in Italy can be found in its capital, Bologna. Its most famous dish that you can get in almost any country is Spaghetti Bolognese, but its title is somewhat of a misnomer. Bolognese sauce, or *ragù,* as it is also known, will taste different wherever you go because there really is no single recipe. The primary ingredients of a Bolognese sauce are chopped meat and tomatoes, but all sorts of variations abound. Here's one that is not too difficult and can be made quickly. After you are familiar with this version, add a few twists to make it your own.

MAKES: *4 servings* • PREPARATION TIME: *30 minutes* • DIFFICULTY: *2*

2 tablespoons extra virgin olive oil
2 tablespoons unsalted butter
1 celery stalk, chopped
1 carrot, chopped
1 sweet onion, chopped

4 ounces pancetta, diced
6 ounces ground veal
6 ounces ground beef
1 28-ounce can crushed tomatoes (see note below)
1 tablespoon sugar
½ cup red wine
2 tablespoons milk or cream
Salt and pepper
Parmesan cheese, grated

Heat oil and butter over medium heat in a large saucepan or skillet. Add celery, carrot, and sweet onion, and sauté for about a minute; then add pancetta and cook for about 2 minutes more. Add veal and beef, and sauté until they turn brown. Add tomato sauce, sugar, and red wine, and stir. Cook over low heat for about 45 minutes; then add milk or cream and cook about 5 minutes more. Season with salt and pepper to taste. Serve over your favorite pasta, passing plenty of Parmesan cheese.

NOTE:

If you prefer, use an equivalent amount of Fresh Tomato Sauce (see p. 77).

28.

Easy All-Purpose White Sauce

Here is an extremely useful sauce you can make in a few minutes and use as a topping for all kinds of pasta and meat dishes. Often, it is mixed with a red sauce, especially in lasagna and heavy pastas. Although the sauce is commonly known by its French name *béchamel,* its actual origin is not known. Food historian Linda Stradley, author of *I'll Have What They're Having: Legendary Local Cuisine,* * believes that the Italian chefs of Catherine de Medici created the sauce, and it was later introduced to the French. Whatever the origin, it is an important ingredient in both Italian (and French) cooking.

MAKES: *4 servings (depending on pasta)* • PREPARATION TIME: *10 minutes* •
DIFFICULTY: *1*

 3 cups milk
 Pinch of nutmeg
 ¼ cup (½ stick) unsalted butter

---

*Linda Stradley, *I'll Have What They're Having: Legendary Local Cuisine* (Kingswood, TX: Falcon Publishing, 2002).

¼ cup all-purpose flour
Salt and pepper

Heat milk over low heat and add nutmeg. Do not boil. In another heavy saucepan, melt butter over low heat. Gradually add the flour to melted butter a few tablespoons at a time, stirring constantly. Add warm milk a little at a time, stirring until smooth and thickened. Sauce should be thick and flowing, but not pasty. Add salt and pepper to taste.

29.

Vodka Sauce

Vodka sauce is a modern Italian American concoction, used on a variety of pastas, but particularly good with penne or cheese ravioli. How the wedding of a hard Russian liquor and an Italian tomato sauce came about is unknown, although some have speculated that a vodka company introduced it in an ad campaign during the 1970s. Still another speculation we've heard is that someone recognized the happy combination of vodka and tomatoes in a Bloody Mary and transferred that insight into making a tomato sauce with vodka. Here's a version you can put together in a snap and have your guests oohing and aahing at the results.

MAKES: *4 servings (depending on pasta)* • PREPARATION TIME: *20 minutes* • DIFFICULTY: *2*

1 teaspoon minced garlic
1 tablespoon olive oil
28-ounce can chopped tomatoes, crushed
¼ pound prosciutto, chopped into small pieces

1 tablespoon fresh parsley, chopped
1 tablespoon crushed bay leaves
1 teaspoon crushed red pepper (optional)
¼ cup vodka
1 cup heavy cream or half and half
½ cup grated Parmesan cheese

Heat oil in skillet and sauté garlic until just light brown. Do not burn. Add crushed tomatoes, prosciutto, parsley, bay leaves, optional red pepper, and vodka, and simmer for about 10 minutes over medium heat. Add heavy cream to sauce and cook for 2 minutes more over low heat. Toss with your favorite cooked pasta and Parmesan cheese. Pass additional Parmesan separately.

30.

Pesto Sauce

Many people think the word "pesto" is a cognate for the English word "paste," but it really means "pounded" and refers not to the texture of the sauce, but rather to the way it is traditionally made. Pesto originated in Genoa. To make it the Genovese way, you need a mortar and pestle, but most modern Italian cooks have no problem making it in a blender or a food processor. There are hundreds of different kinds of pesto—made from ingredients like parsley, basil, pine nuts, garlic, olive oil, walnuts, Parmesan cheese, and other mixtures of nuts, herbs, oil, and cheese. This recipe makes a kind of pure Genovese pesto, allowing the flavors of garlic, basil, pine nuts, olive oil, and cheese to blend but retain their individual taste as well.

MAKES: *enough sauce for 4 servings of pasta* • PREPARATION TIME: *10 minutes* • DIFFICULTY: *2*

2 cups loosely packed fresh basil leaves, coarsely chopped
2 medium garlic cloves
1 teaspoon salt

3 ounces pine nuts
2 tablespoons plus grated Parmesan cheese for serving
1 cup extra virgin olive oil

In a blender or food processor, mix the basil, garlic, salt, pine nuts, Parmesan, and ½ cup of the olive oil at medium speed. Blend just until the pesto has a grainy texture—do not puree completely because a good pesto has a very distinctive texture. It is never mushy or too liquid. While you're blending, scrape the mixture from the sides a few times and continue mixing. Spoon mixture into a sealable container, add the remaining olive oil, and blend with a spatula until all the oil is absorbed. To store, seal container after a layer of oil has formed or add a few more drops of oil to cover. Seal tightly and store in refrigerator for up to two weeks.

When ready to serve, bring to room temperature. Add your favorite pasta to a large pot of boiling water until al dente. Drain in a colander and mix pesto with pasta in serving bowl until well coated. Serve immediately, passing additional Parmesan separately.

31.

Spaghetti with Mama's "Sunday Sauce"

Sunday dinner is a special time in Italian households and is usually a chance for the entire family to sit down together and enjoy a hearty meal. Often it consists of a tomato-based sauce, stewed with various flavorful meats and served over warm pasta. It is more elaborate than a standard sauce and can take hours to prepare. Somewhere along the way, the day became synonymous with the meal, and the term "Sunday Sauce" was coined. This version comes from the owner-chef Joe Busalacchi's San Diego restaurant, Po Pazzo (which means "A Little Bit Crazy"). It may take you all day, but we promise that you will never regret the time you spend making it. Serve it for your own family on a Sunday and enjoy everyone's satisfied expressions after the meal.

This recipe requires several subrecipes: meat sauce, meat balls, and short ribs and sausage. Also, it is actually better to use dried pasta, as fresh pasta will get too mushy under heavy sauce. Follow the recipes below to prepare the sauce, meatballs, and, ribs and sausages. Keep warm adding additional marinara sauce if necessary.

MAKES: *4 servings* • PREPARATION TIME: *2 hours or more* • DIFFICULTY: *3*

THE MEAT SAUCE:
¼ cup olive oil
1 pound ground beef, lean
1 white onion, chopped
1 carrot, peeled and chopped
2 celery ribs, chopped
2 28-ounce cans crushed tomatoes
Salt and pepper

THE MEATBALLS:
1 pound ground beef, 95% lean
½ white onion, finely chopped
¾ cup Italian bread crumbs
1 tablespoon mixed fresh herbs (rosemary, oregano, parsley, basil),
    finely chopped
½ cup grated Parmesan cheese
Salt and pepper

THE BEEF SHORT RIBS AND SAUSAGE:
4 beef short ribs
4 Italian sausage links, mild
1 28-ounce jar marinara sauce, premium quality

LAST 3 INGREDIENTS ARE FOR THE SPAGHETTI:
1 pound dried spaghetti (see note, p. 90)
Salt and pepper
Parmesan cheese, grated

To prepare meat sauce: Heat olive oil in a large skillet; then add meat and cook until brown. Remove meat from skillet and drain on plate covered with paper towels and set aside. Drain fat from skillet; then add fresh chopped onion, carrot, and celery ribs to same skillet and cook until soft. Add crushed canned tomatoes to vegetables and blend. Add meat to vegetable mixture in skillet. Season with salt and pepper to taste and cook on low heat for about 20 minutes or until sauce is neither too runny nor too dry. Keep warm on very low heat.

To prepare meat balls: Heat oven to 400 degrees. Combine all ingredients and form into ping-pong-sized balls. Place in small baking dish and cook in the oven for 20 minutes or until nicely browned. Remove from oven and set aside.

To prepare beef short ribs and sausage: Sear the ribs in a very large skillet until deeply browned on all sides. Add sausage to skillet and brown, turning several times. Add three quarters of jar of marinara sauce and braise over very low heat for 15–20 minutes; then remove sausage, set aside, and continue to braise ribs 1 hour or more until tender. (Meat should easily fall off the bone.) If sauce is evaporating, add some water or red wine to be sure ribs are covered. When ribs are done, add sausage and meatballs to the skillet, cover with additional marinara sauce, cook for about 10 minutes more, and then keep warm over very low heat.

In a large pot, cook the spaghetti according to directions in boiling salted water until al dente. Strain and add to the warm meat sauce. Reduce the sauce slightly until it tastes right to you; then season with salt and pepper. Divide the pasta and sauce among four plates, and surround each with a meatball, a short rib, and sausage. Top with Parmesan.

NOTE:

If available, preferably use DeCecco, Ronzoni, or Barrilla dried spaghetti.

32.

Fusilli with Olives, Peas, and Pecorino
Fusilli con Olive, Piselli, e Pecorino

"This dish is the marriage of three wonderful flavors: the salty chunks of olive, the delicate taste of sweet pea, the finish of sharp pecorino," says Piero Selvaggio, owner of the Los Angeles and Las Vegas' famed Valentino Restaurants.

Pecorino is a sheep's milk cheese, not as creamy and sweet as Parmesan, but saltier and more masculine. This recipe is typical of southern Italy—strong flavors, but intriguing in the mouth, especially if you match it to a nice robust wine. It's a very intense and satisfying dish.

MAKES: *4 servings* • PREPARATION TIME: *45 minutes* • DIFFICULTY: *3*

1 pound fusilli
½ cup olive oil
1 cup fresh peas, steamed until tender
1 pound raw spinach, steamed and chopped
Salt and pepper
2 whole garlic cloves
Red crushed chili peppers (optional)

¼ cup dry white wine
5 fresh basil leaves, finely chopped
½ cup chopped imported black olives
½ cup grated aged pecorino cheese

In a large pot of boiling, salted water, cook the fusilli until just al dente. Drain and toss with 1 tablespoon of the oil to keep the pasta from sticking. Set aside to cool.

Combine half of the peas and half of the spinach with 5 tablespoons of the olive oil and put into a food processor. Puree until smooth. Salt and pepper to taste, and set aside.

Brown the garlic with the remaining olive oil in a large skillet over medium heat. Discard the garlic. Add the chili flakes (if using) and sauté. Add the wine and cook until evaporated, about 2–3 minutes. Add the remaining peas, spinach, and basil, and sauté another minute. Season to taste and set aside to cool.

In a large bowl, combine the pasta, sautéed vegetables, olives, three quarters of the pureed vegetables, and pecorino cheese, and toss well. Add more vegetable puree if needed. Serve within 3–4 hours at room temperature.

33.

Rigatoni with Ricotta

This well-known pasta is often the *prima piatto* (first course) at many Italian-American family dinners. As usual, the freshness of the ingredients is key. For us, this is a kind of unadulterated Italian "soul food"—straightforward, delicious, and comforting. The texture is chewy, the flavor is summer itself, and the afterglow is utterly satisfying.

MAKES: *4 servings* • PREPARATION TIME: *30 minutes* • DIFFICULTY: *1*

1 pound rigatoni, penne, or other tubular pasta
3 tablespoons extra virgin olive oil
1 small onion, minced
1 tablespoon chopped parsley
2 cups Fresh Tomato Sauce (p. 77) or premium prepared marinara sauce
Salt
½ pound fresh whole milk ricotta

Boil rigatoni in salted water until al dente. Drain. Heat olive oil in large skillet. Sauté onion and parsley over low heat until onion is translucent. Add tomato sauce to skillet, salt to taste, and cook for 15 minutes. Add rigatoni and ricotta to skillet and toss until ricotta is well mixed with pasta and tomato sauce.

34.

Penne alla Giulietta

The D'Alo family, owners of Trattoria La Siciliana in Berkeley, California, contributed this delightful penne recipe, one of their most popular dishes. Rosa and Giuseppe D'Alo were born and raised in Palermo, Sicily, and when they came to America, they brought their passion for cooking with them. They also bestowed their gifts on their children. Now, Angelo and Jerry D'Alo are the executive chefs, and every dish that comes out of their tiny kitchen is a work of "passion, art, and love," says Giulia D'Alo, the third-generation D'Alo, for which this recipe was named.

MAKES: *4 servings* • PREPARATION TIME: *30 minutes* • DIFFICULTY: *2*

Salt
1 pound penne rigate
½ cup olive oil
½ to whole clove of fresh garlic
Salt and pepper
2 large whole tomatoes, crushed (do not strain)

    3 tablespoons chopped fresh basil
    1 pound shredded high-quality mozzarella (see note)
    1 small pinch dried oregano

Bring 6 quarts of water to a boil with salt and 1 tablespoon of the oil. Add the penne and cook for 7 to 9 minutes until al dente. Strain and save 2 ounces of the boiled pasta water. Return pasta to the same pot with the saved water.

While pasta is cooking, prepare the sauce. Heat the remaining olive oil in a medium skillet and sauté one-half or whole garlic (to taste) until golden. Add salt and pepper to taste, tomatoes, and 2 tablespoons of the fresh basil and continue to sauté. Add half of the mozzarella to skillet and keep warm. Add the sauce as well as the remaining mozzarella and basil to the pasta, and mix well. Drizzle with additional olive oil and sprinkle with oregano just before serving.

NOTE:

If available, use mozzarella di bufala.

35.

Spaghettini with Garlic and Olive Oil
Spaghettini all' Aglio e Olio

Speaking to the graduating class at Rutgers University, the celebrity chef Mario Batali (television's "Molto Mario") offered the graduates some very useful advice. He urged them to seek honest, passionate, and intense experiences and to forget about following the rules. "You want a recipe?" he asked. "Boil some spaghetti in well-salted water. While you're doing that, heat up some good extra virgin olive oil in a skillet and throw in some thick slices of garlic and some red pepper flakes. When the pasta's cooked, toss it around. Put it on a plate. Grate some Parmigiano-Reggiano on top. Congratulations, dude. You've just made *spaghetti all' aglio*."

We like to add some chopped parsley to our version and simmer the pasta (after it's cooked very al dente, cooked but firm) in chicken broth. So if you need rules, here's our own recipe for *pasta all' aglio e olio* that you can make whenever the spirit moves you.

MAKES: *4 servings* • PREPARATION TIME: *25 minutes* • DIFFICULTY: *2*

1 pound dried spaghettini (see note, p. 98)

Salt
⅓ cup extra virgin olive oil
6 garlic cloves, peeled and sliced
1 cup of chicken broth (½ of an 8 ounce can)
6 garlic cloves, peeled and minced
4 tablespoons chopped parsley
Red pepper flakes
½ cup freshly grated Parmesan cheese

Add the pasta in a large pot filled with salted water. While it's boiling, heat 2 tablespoons of the oil in a large skillet and sauté the six sliced garlic cloves over medium-low heat until light brown. Do not let the garlic turn dark. Remove skillet from heat, add remaining olive oil and set aside.

After just a few minutes, drain the pasta in a colander and pour the chicken broth into the empty pasta pot. Bring broth to a boil and return the al dente pasta to the pot until the boiling broth nearly evaporates. When the broth is nearly gone, remove the pot from the heat and add the six uncooked, minced garlic cloves and parsley to the spaghettini.

Toss the mixture a few times; then add the spaghettini to the skillet and toss with the olive oil and sliced garlic. Sprinkle with red pepper flakes to taste and toss with Parmesan cheese. Serve immediately.

NOTE:

If available, use dried Di Cecco, Barilla, or Ronzoni Spaghettini.

36.

Orecchiette with Potatoes and Arugula

Pasta and potatoes together may seem a bit starchy to the American palate, but this dish blends them seamlessly and makes the pasta taste almost like gnocchi. Orecchiette means "little ears," and that's how this pasta is shaped. It's a specialty in various parts of southern Italy, especially in Apulia, the heel of the Italian boot where our own family originated. We got this recipe years ago from cousin Cesita who was a wonderful cook and could turn an ordinary meal into a feast.

MAKES: *4 servings* • PREPARATION TIME: *15 minutes* • DIFFICULTY: *1*

1 large bunch arugula
1 pound Yukon Gold potatoes, peeled and sliced in ¼-inch pieces
Salt
1 pound orecchiette
1 garlic clove, minced
1 dry hot red pepper, chopped (wear rubber gloves) (see note)
3 tablespoons extra virgin olive oil

Wash arugula and boil with potatoes in salted water. After five minutes, add orecchiette and cook until al dente (follow package directions). Drain. Heat oil in large skillet and sauté garlic and red pepper (or pepper flakes) for about 2 minutes. Add cooked pasta, potatoes, and arugula to the skillet and salt to taste. Toss all ingredients and serve.

NOTE:

If you want to make it less hot, leave out this ingredient and add a few pinches of red pepper flakes.

37.

Cavatelli with White Beans and Mussels

The small seaside village of Monopoli in Apulia is not far from Trulli country, those famous round conical-roofed houses that dot the landscape of the village of Alberobello and its vicinity. Il Melograno, a well-known resort there, is a family-operated hotel run for many years by the Guerra family. The impressive parklike setting of Il Melograno is dotted with olive and citrus trees, and it is a wonderful ambience in which to dine al fresco. We visited there a few years ago and had this lovely pasta dish prepared by Chef Stefano Tagliente on a brilliant July day at the lovely outdoor terrace restaurant overlooking the hotel's pool. Heaven did not seem very distant.

MAKES: *6 servings* • PREPARATION TIME: *30 minutes (beans soaked overnight)* • DIFFICULTY: *3*

12 ounces dried white beans (for soaking, see note, p. 68)
3 ounces cherry tomatoes
1 celery rib, cut into ¼-inch slices
1 carrot, peeled and sliced

    1 bay leaf
    1½ pounds mussels
    ½ cup extra virgin olive oil
    4 garlic cloves, minced
    1 small bunch Italian parsley, chopped
    1 hot red pepper, cut into thirds (wear rubber gloves)
    12 ounces cavatelli pasta (see note 1 below)

After you have soaked the beans overnight change water and bring them to a boil, adding tomatoes, celery, carrot, and bay leaf. Cook about one hour until tender.

Open the mussels (see note 2), trim "beards" (see note 3) and keep any water in them. Brown the garlic over medium heat in a large skillet with half the olive oil. Add mussels and their water, parsley, and hot pepper.

Cook cavatelli in a large pot of boiling water until al dente. Drain and add to skillet. Toss in beans and sauté all ingredients for two minutes. Discard bay leaf. Add the remaining olive oil and serve immediately.

NOTES:

1. Cavatelli pasta is available at many Italian markets and in some supermarkets

2. Wash and scrub mussel shells to get rid of grit. Debeard mussels, and place in cold water, cover, and steam until shells open. *Discard any closed mussels.*

3. Mussels have a stingy beard protruding from the crack between the two shells that you pull to remove. *Do not debeard* until you are ready to cook, because debearding and setting aside may cause the mussels to die.

38.

Spaghetti Carbonara

"Growing up in the Moramarco household, one of my favorite dishes to cook was spaghetti carbonara," remembers Nicholas, Federico's other son and Stephen's brother. "Why? Well, not only was it delicious, but it was very easy for a kid to make." But don't let that lead you astray; a good spaghetti carbonara takes a little love and care. Classic carbonara contains only bacon, pasta and eggs—there is no cream. If you're not a cook or you're teaching a family member how to make pasta, this is an excellent recipe for someone's first time. Some people use whole eggs instead of yolks alone, but we prefer this version because it's less runny and the golden hue of the sauce is more pleasing to the eye.

MAKES: *4 servings* • PREPARATION TIME: *15 minutes* • DIFFICULTY: *1*

    8 slices pancetta (or any thick-cut bacon)
    2 tablespoons olive oil
    1 glove clove, finely chopped
    8 egg yolks

Salt and pepper
1 pound spaghetti
¼ cup parsley, chopped fine
Freshly grated Parmesan cheese

Chop bacon into 1-inch squares. Heat oil in a medium skillet over medium heat, adding the bacon and garlic when hot. Cook bacon slowly, allowing it to get crispy, but not burnt. Remove from heat.

In a bowl, beat egg yolks, add salt and pepper, and let stand.

While bacon is cooking, boil water, break pasta in half, and add to water. Cook for about 8 minutes until it's chewy. Remove from heat, drain, and place in large bowl.

Add egg yolks, parsley, bacon, and garlic to the pasta and mix vigorously. The eggs are actually cooked by the warm pasta, so make sure they are thoroughly mixed. Add salt and pepper to taste. Top with grated Parmesan.

39.

Pasta with Sardines, Anchovies, and Fennel Sauce

Pasta cu Sardi e Finocchio

Pasta with sardines and anchovies is one of the staples of the Sicilian diet. These salty fish are an acquired taste, and may not be for everyone, but live dangerously and give it a try.

This is another recipe from the Di Fiore family cookbook. This dish is a personal favorite of Vincent Di Fiore, as he remembers making it with his father after they picked wild fennel on the peninsula, during a family trip to his hometown. Vincent is an accomplished musician, playing trumpet and keyboards in the world-famous pop group Cake.

MAKES: *4 servings* • PREPARATION TIME: *20 minutes* • DIFFICULTY: *2*

Large bunch of tender fennel greens
2 tablespoons olive oil
1 medium onion, diced
1 can anchovies, drained
1 can sardines, drained and diced
2 heaping tablespoons of pine nuts (pignoli)

Salt and pepper
Spaghetti or perciatelli (see note below)

Boil the fennel greens in a large pot of water until tender. Remove and cut up into small pieces with scissors or chop in blender or food processor. Save the water.

Heat oil in a medium skillet and sauté the onion and anchovies. Add the sardines, pine nuts, and salt and pepper to taste. Add the cut-up fennel to the sardine mixture with a little of the saved water from the fennel to make the desired consistency. This is the "sauce" for the pasta. Simmer until the pasta is ready.

Boil the pasta in the remaining saved fennel water. Drain the pasta, mix in a little of the sauce, and stir. Serve each individual pasta dish with more of the fennel sauce on top.

NOTE:

Perciatelli is like spaghetti, but with a pinhole through the strand, which helps absorb the sauce.

40.
Pasta with Zucchini

Santino Giametta lived until he was ninety-five years old, always cultivating a full-scale Italian-style garden in the backyard of his San Diego home. His longevity can certainly be attributed to the healthy food he grew and ate in sunny Southern California. We met Santino in the last years of his life when writing a story about Italian gardeners for a local paper, and we include the recipe he gave us as a tribute to him and Italian gardeners everywhere.

MAKES: *4 servings* • PREPARATION TIME: *40 minutes* • DIFFICULTY: *2*

    1 onion, peeled and finely chopped
    2 garlic cloves, peeled and minced
    2 tablespoons extra virgin olive oil
    1½ cups tomatoes chopped, and crushed, fresh (see p. 77) or
        home canned, if possible
    Salt and pepper
    3 medium zucchini, peeled, quartered lengthwise, and cut into ½-
        inch pieces

1 pound linguini fini or spaghettini
Grated ricotta salata or Parmesan cheese

Heat oil in a skillet over medium-low heat and sauté onions and garlic until onions are translucent. Add crushed tomatoes, mix, turn heat to low and simmer. Sprinkle with salt and pepper to taste. When sauce has simmered for 20 minutes add zucchini and cook for 8–10 minutes more until it is tender. While zucchini and sauce are simmering, break pasta into three pieces and add to the boiling salted water. Boil until al dente—about 6 or 7 minutes or according to package directions. Do not overcook. Drain pasta in colander and transfer to serving plate. Cover with sauce and toss to mix thoroughly. Sprinkle with cheese to taste and serve.

41.
Fettucini with Arugula and Goat Cheese

Antonino Mastellone is the owner of a number of highly regarded San Diego restaurants, but the one we like best is the first one he opened here in the late 1990s called Arrivederci. It's a casual, comfortable place with a little front terrace where you can nibble on appetizers, drink a few glasses of wine, and "people watch" for hours. Here's a unique pasta dish from their menu that you won't find in many other Italian restaurants.

MAKES: *4 servings* • PREPARATION TIME: *20 minutes* • DIFFICULTY: *2*

1 pound dry fettucini
4 tablespoons onions, chopped fine
3 cloves garlic, minced
2 cups Roma tomatoes, diced
3 tablespoons extra virgin olive oil
½ cup white wine
4 cups tomato sauce, homemade (see p. 77) or your favorite
   bottled variety

    1 cup heavy whipping cream
    Salt and pepper
    1 cup tightly packed arugula, tough stems removed
    4 ounces goat cheese
    Parmesan cheese

In a large pot, cook fettucini according to package directions until al dente. Drain and set aside. In a large skillet, sauté onions, garlic, and tomatoes in olive oil until onions are translucent and tomatoes are soft. Deglaze (see p. 7) with white wine.

Add tomato sauce and cream, and reduce until sauce is thickened. Season with salt and pepper to taste.

Add fettucini and arugula, and toss to mix and slightly wilt arugula. Transfer to individual pasta bowls and top with crumbled goat cheese and Parmesan. Serve immediately.

42.

Troccoli, Foggia-Style

Troccoli is a type of spaghetti, popular in the Apulia region of Italy, where the Moramarco family originates. While there are many variations of troccoli, it is essentially a thick, square pasta that is chewier than regular spaghetti. This recipe was given to us by Roberto Cicolella, owner of Cicolella in Fiera, in the provincial town of Foggia, when we were there visiting family. Apulians believe in the immediacy of their dishes. "*Dal tierra, al tavola*—from the earth to the table," Roberto told us, almost as a mantra. In other words, the fresher the ingredients, the better this meal will taste.

MAKES: *4 servings* • PREPARATION TIME: *1 hour* • DIFFICULTY: *2*

2 teaspoons salt
¼ cup olive oil
1¾ ounces pancetta (nonsmoked)
1 onion, chopped
8 ounces brown Italian mushrooms, sliced
2 teaspoons parsley, chopped

    2 tablespoons basil, chopped
½ glass white wine
1 quart tomato puree, store-bought
1 pound troccoli (or any thick, spaghetti-like pasta)
Pecorino or Parmesan cheese

Boil salted water for pasta in a large saucepan. While waiting for the water to boil, heat olive oil in a large skillet. Sauté the pancetta with the onion until the latter is soft and translucent. Add mushrooms and continue to sauté for several minutes, adding parsley, basil, and white wine. When wine evaporates, add the tomato puree and simmer over very low heat for about 45 minutes or until the sauce thickens. Just before the sauce is done, cook the pasta in the salted water, drain, and transfer to a large serving dish. Top with sauce and sprinkle with pecorino or Parmesan cheese.

43.

Foie Gras Gnocchi

Along the famous Charles Street corridor in Baltimore, resides Sotto Sopra, an Italian restaurant that specializes in diversity. Owner Riccardo Bosio came up with an ingenious method of keeping the menu fresh: every eighteen months, the restaurant interchanges chefs from a group of the best Italian chefs in the region.

This particular recipe comes from Chef Paolo Santianami who has taken a traditional potato-based pasta and married it with perhaps one of the most sinful yet delicious delicacies on the planet, combining a peasant food—gnocchi—with such haute cuisine ingredients as foie gras and truffles.

MAKES: *4 servings* • PREPARATION TIME: *2 hours* • DIFFICULTY: *4*

Special equipment: parchment paper

FOR THE GNOCCHI DOUGH:
2¼ pounds boiled potatoes (skin on)
1¾ cups all-purpose flour

2 extra large eggs
Salt and Pepper

For Gnocchi:
7 ounces foie gras (available in specialty or gourmet shops)
2 tablespoons flour

For the Sauce:
¼ pound unsalted butter
2–3 fresh sage leaves
2 cups heavy cream
5 ounces grated Parmesan cheese

Plum tomatoes for garnish
Black or white truffle for garnish (optional)

To prepare gnocchi dough: Wash the potatoes and boil skin on. When cooked, drain from the water, let cool a bit, remove the skins and chill in the refrigerator for about 10 minutes. Place the potatoes in a food processor combined with flour, eggs, and salt and pepper to taste until the consistency of the dough is reached. (Test a piece of the dough by sticking your finger in it— your fingerprint should remain in the dough, not spring back.)

To assemble gnocchi: Take about 2 inches of dough—start to roll as if making a meatball—and insert a cube of the foie gras inside ball. To complete the rolling process, seal all around the ball. No foie gras should be showing through the dough.

Place the balls on a sheet pan covered with floured parchment paper—then place in the freezer until hard. (They will stay fresh in the freezer for about 30 days.)

When you're ready to prepare, it's important to keep them frozen. Place frozen gnocchi in boiling, salted water for about 3–4 minutes until gnocchi rise to the top. Remove with slotted spoon and strain.

To prepare the sauce: In a small skillet, sauté gnocchi in butter and sage leaves. Simmer cream and Parmesan in a separate saucepan.

Place crème sauce on the bottom of a plate. Carefully place each gnocchi (8–10 per serving) on top of the crème sauce. To garnish, take the chopped fresh plum tomatoes cut small in a dice, and if you're feeling especially extravagant, add optional shaved black or white truffle to taste.

NOTE:

Foie gras is available in specialty or gourmet shops and in some grocery stores.

44.

Fettucini Alfredo

This classic Roman dish was invented in the early twentieth century, at Alfredo De Lelio's restaurant. Legend has it that Alfredo invented the dish to reawaken his wife's appetite after she gave birth. The dish gained worldwide fame after legendary movie stars Douglas Fairbanks and Mary Pickford fell in love with it when visiting Rome.

Alfredo had good instincts, because his version of fettucini is an extraordinarily rich pasta, and it will stir and stimulate even the most tired palate. It is best served in small portions as a first course.

MAKES: *4 servings* • PREPARATION TIME: *20 minutes* • DIFFICULTY: *2*

1 teaspoon salt
1 pound fresh fettucini (see Homemade Fresh Pasta, p. 73, or buy
    ready-made in an Italian deli)
½ cup heavy cream
3 tablespoons European butter (see note 1, p. 118)
Salt and pepper

¼ teaspoon freshly ground nutmeg
1 cup freshly grated Parmesan cheese

Bring salted water to a boil in a large pot. Warm four pasta bowls in low-heat oven or fill with boiling water and keep warm. Add pasta to the salted boiling water and cook until just shy of al dente. Drain in colander. Mix cream and butter in a large skillet over medium-low heat, stirring constantly. Add pasta to cream mixture, season with salt and pepper to taste, sprinkle with nutmeg and Parmesan, and toss. Divide pasta among warmed serving bowls and serve immediately (see note 2).

NOTES:

1. European butter is available in gourmet and specialty shops. It usually contains 82 percent to 84 percent butterfat, is unsalted, and is referred to as dry butter because of its low water content.

2. Alfredo sauce gets lumpy as it cools, so it's best to serve it in warmed bowls. If served as a main course, sprinkle the finished pasta with chopped up bits of prosciutto, toss, and serve.

45

Grandma's Four-Cheese Ravioli
Ravioli Quattro Formaggio

Homemade ravioli is not a dish to make casually. It requires time, attention, and care, but the result is well worth it. We devoted the better part of a day to making this recipe, which comes from our friend Dan Venzoni, who passed on his mom's secrets to us. At the end of the day, the house looked like it had been hit by a flour tornado, but we invited some friends to join us and taste our creations, and it was, to quote Shakespeare's Osric, "A hit, a very palpable hit."

MAKES: *6 servings* • PREPARATION TIME: *2–3 hours* • DIFFICULTY: *5*

Special equipment: ravioli or pizza cutter

FOR THE PASTA:
Homemade Fresh Pasta (see p. 73)
Flour, all purpose, add as needed

FOR THE FILLING

2 pounds fresh ricotta (whole milk)
8 ounces grated Parmesan cheese
4 ounces Romano or Asiago cheese (or 2 ounces of each)
1 pound mozzarella cheese, shredded
1 14-ounce package frozen chopped spinach
¼ cup parsley, chopped fine
¾ teaspoon salt
2 eggs
Pinch of nutmeg
Pepper

To prepare the pasta: Follow directions for Homemade Fresh Pasta (pp. 73–76) adding half eggshell of water as indicated.

Lay 15- by 4-inch wide strips of pasta (rolled to the thinnest setting on a pasta machine) on a well-floured surface. (Very important—use more flour rather than less.)

To prepare the filling and to assemble ravioli: Mix all filling ingredients in a large bowl with pepper to taste. Mound approximately one tablespoon of the mixture, two inches apart in the center of each strip, fold pasta over, and cut into individual ravioli with a ravioli cutter, about 5 to 6 per strip. Seal each ravioli closed with the tines of a fork and let dry on a tray.

Freeze tray for 10–15 minutes (or longer if you plan to cook later) until ravioli are firm. While ravioli are in freezer, bring a large pot of water to a boil.

Then add ravioli to water and cook until al dente (cooked but firm), about 8 minutes or until all ravioli rise to the surface. Drain in colander and serve with your favorite sauce.

NOTE:

This is especially good with Vodka Sauce (p. 83) or with a tomato sauce mixed with a little béchamel sauce (Easy All-Purpose White Sauce, p. 81).

46

Crabmeat Ravioli

Many ways are available to make a good ravioli, and here is another, filled with succulent crab. This is the signature dish of La Rivera Restaurant, located in Metairie, Louisiana. La Rivera was founded in 1969 by Chef Goffredo Fraccaro, originally from Tortona, Italy,

Goffredo has been consistently amazing Louisianans and tantalizing their taste buds with inventive recipes from calamari to osso buco. He is the only Italian chef to win a Gold Medal at the Crabmeat Olympics in San Francisco with this very recipe, so you know it's got to be good!

MAKES: *6 servings* • PREPARATION TIME: *1 hour, 30 minutes* • DIFFICULTY: *5*

Special equipment: ravioli or pizza cutter

FOR THE CRABMEAT FILLING:
1 pound lump crabmeat
½ cup heavy cream, reduced by one third
Salt and pepper

2 ounces softened butter
1 tablespoon butter
½ cup minced green onion
½ cup unsalted cracker crumbs

FOR THE RAVIOLI DOUGH:
2⅔ cups all-purpose flour
4 eggs, slightly beaten
4 tablespoons oil or clarified butter (see note)
4 tablespoons water

FOR THE RAVIOLI SAUCE:
1 cup whipping cream, reduce by half
½ stick (¼ cup) butter
Red pepper flakes
½ cup freshly grated Parmesan cheese

To prepare the crabmeat filling: Pick over crabmeat for any excess shell pieces. Pour cream into heavy saucepan, reduce by one-third and season with salt and pepper. Whisk in the softened butter. Add the picked crabmeat to the sauce. Melt 1 tablespoon butter in another pan and sauté green onion until clear but not browned. Add onion and cracker crumbs to crabmeat mixture and combine. Refrigerate to cool while you prepare the dough for the ravioli.

To prepare the ravioli dough: Put the flour in a large bowl and add eggs, oil or butter, and water. Work with hands or a wooden spoon until thoroughly mixed and dough forms a ball. Knead for 5 or 6 minutes. Set in bowl to rest, for about one hour.

On a floured board or other smooth surface, roll dough until it is paper thin. (You will need two sheets to form the ravioli.) Shape crabmeat filling into balls the size of a large marble. Place them about 1½ inches apart on one sheet of the pasta dough. Cover with second sheet.

Bring medium pot of salted water to a rapid boil. While waiting for water to boil, form ravioli by pressing around each ball to form a seal. Dust with flour and cut into squares with a ravioli or pizza cutter. Put ravioli in rapidly boiling water and cook for 5 minutes. Drain.

To prepare the sauce: Bring cream to a low boil, and blend in the butter. Top ravioli with sauce, sprinkle with parsley, red pepper flakes (optional) and grated Parmesan cheese.

NOTE:

Clarified butter is heated, unsalted butter with the water and milk solids removed. It forms three layers. The top layer is foam, and it should be skimmed off with a spoon. The milk solids drop to the bottom. The middle layer is clarified butter. Allow butter to sit for a few minutes; then either strain through cheesecloth-lined strainer or fine sieve or gently pour off butter from the milk solids, leaving clarified butter (butterfat).

47.
Tagliatelle Porcini

This recipe is from the province of Parma, where the best porcini mushrooms are grown. To be exact, the actual town that you get the best of the best is Borgo Val Di Taro. The reason for this, according to Joseph Bicocchi, former owner of the Grifone Restaurant in New York City, is that they grow under the chestnut trees and absorb an acid that is commonly known as *tanino*. During the fall months is the best time to get these mushrooms, but fresh or dried, they have a unique nutty flavor that makes any dish they are added to earthy and distinctive.

MAKES: *4 servings* • PREPARATION TIME: *20 minutes* • DIFFICULTY: *3*

FOR THE SAUCE:
Salt
1 cup dry porcini mushrooms
3 cups chicken broth
½ cup olive oil
2 shallots, peeled and chopped fine

3 tablespoons chopped Italian *pancetta arrotolata* (this is the
   "rolled" style of pancetta, chopped)
1 cup tomato sauce (no garlic)

¾ pound fresh tagliatelle or fettucine
½ cup grated Parmesan or pecorino cheese

Bring a large pot of lightly salted water to a boil.

To prepare the sauce: Soak porcini in chicken broth for about 15 minutes. Do not oversoak. Heat olive oil in a medium skillet and sauté shallots until golden in color. Add pancetta. When golden, drain oil. Strain porcini, add to tomato sauce and add both to skillet. Let simmer until sauce is on the thick side and keep warm.

Add fetuccini or tagliatelle to boiling water. When, al dente, serve with porcini sauce and grated cheese.

Rice and Polenta

RISO E POLENTA

There are at least fifty varieties of rice grown in Italy, and in many regions it is as basic a staple of the Italian diet as pasta. It is also prepared with many different kinds of sauces and toppings. Perhaps the most famous Italian rice dish is Risotto Milanese, which is to the city of Milan what Spaghetti Bolognese is to Bologna. Risotto *does not mean rice, however, but refers to the specific way that dish is prepared, absorbing the liquid slowly and giving the rice a creamy texture. A good risotto is made from Italian arborio rice, a plump grain that becomes both creamy and chewy when it is cooked in a broth. Carnaroli rice is also a popular choice, but it can be hard to find. Risotto and polenta (simply cooked cornmeal) are both substitutes for pasta in various regions of Italy.*

Polenta is generally more popular in the north of Italy—in Lombardy, Liguria, and Veneto—although many versions are served throughout the country. Either rice or polenta makes a satisfying alternative to the beginning of an Italian meal and can broaden your culinary repertoire considerably.

48.

Rice with Radicchio and Taleggio Cheese

Risotto alla Valtellina

Taleggio is a soft cheese that is tangy when young and becomes fuller in flavor as it ages. Its creamy texture makes it an excellent additive to a risotto, as this recipe from Aldo and Louise Blasi, owners of Ristorante Milano in San Francisco, shows.

Aldo Blasi is also a wine expert with over twenty-five years of experience, and he suggests pairing this dish with a red wine from a vineyard in the Langhe of northern Italy, Cogno, Montegrili, 2000. A mix of Nebbiolo and Barbera grapes, this wine is ruby red, elegant, with a long lasting finish and fresh palate.

MAKES: *4 servings* • PREPARATION TIME: *25 minutes* • DIFFICULTY: *3*

About 5 cups of vegetable broth
1 medium radicchio
2 tablespoons unsalted butter
1 tablespoon olive oil
1 large yellow onion, finely chopped
1 cup of arborio rice

½ cup dry white wine
¼ pound taleggio cheese, cubed, rind removed
Salt and pepper

Pour broth into small saucepan and keep on simmer. Cut radicchio into strips. In a larger saucepan, melt butter with olive oil over medium heat. Add the onion and radicchio and sauté slowly until tender. Add rice, stirring constantly with a wooden spoon until grains are thoroughly coated. Add the wine and continue stirring until liquid is absorbed.

Add the simmering stock one ladle at a time, stirring constantly. Make sure the liquid is absorbed before adding more. When rice is partially cooked, add talleggio cheese.

Risotto is done when the grains are still a bit firm but tender, the consistency creamy. It takes about 20–25 minutes, and the amount of broth you need may vary. Add salt and pepper to taste before serving.

49.

Risotto Milanese

Risotto Milanese is a classic Italian recipe featuring saffron, a very expensive spice made from the stamen of a crocus flower. The mythic origins of this dish date to the sixteenth century when allegedly an artist from Milan was inspired to add this gold-hued herb, originally used for tinting paint, to a dish of rice for his daughter's wedding.

Although, as in most Italian cooking, there are many variations on the dish, this basic version is quite easy to make. The key is to stir constantly over medium-low heat with a wooden spoon and add neither too much nor too little broth to the saucepan at a time—only as much as can be absorbed in a couple of minutes.

MAKES: *4 servings* • PREPARATION TIME: *30 minutes* • DIFFICULTY LEVEL: *3*

- 1 tablespoon olive oil
- 4 tablespoon butter
- 1 small onion, finely chopped
- 2 cups arborio rice

4–6 cups of broth (beef, chicken, vegetable, or fish)
⅔ cup Parmesan cheese, grated
1 teaspoon saffron threads

Heat oil and butter in a large, flat-bottomed skillet over medium-low heat. Add the diced onion and cook until the onion is translucent. Please, *do not wash rice before cooking or it will wash away the starch*. Add rice, stirring constantly with a wooden spoon until the kernels are covered in butter and turn slightly brown. Turn heat to low.

Begin by slowly adding broth a little at a time while stirring the rice. Once the broth has been absorbed, add more. The trick is not to let the rice get too dry or to let it drown in broth. Before rice has finished cooking, about ten minutes into the process, add optional ingredients (see variations) and continue to stir. Once broth is all used, or after about 20 minutes, add Parmesan cheese and saffron, again stirring constantly until the cheese is blended and saffron turns the rice a golden color.

Remove from heat and cover for 3–4 minutes. Then, serve immediately.

VARIATIONS: To expand the dish try ¼ cup prosciutto, mushrooms, shrimp, or other vegetable/seafood of your choice, finely chopped. Use broth to match the addition.

50.
Risotto Frutti di Mare

It wouldn't be right to have a book called *Deliciously Italian* without including something from New York's Little Italy, so here's an aromatic and succulent fish and rice dish from Il Cortile Restaurant on Mulberry Street. When Italian immigrants first arrived in this country at the turn of the twentieth century, many of them settled together in neighborhoods, this Lower Manhattan area being the most famous. It's a popular tourist destination and is still one of the best places in New York to get a good, classic Italian meal.

MAKES: *4 servings* • PREPARATION TIME: *45 minutes* • DIFFICULTY: *4*

Special equipment: cheese cloth

FOR THE FISH BROTH:
1 quart water
6 clams
6 mussels
1 sprig rosemary

6 leaves sage
1 bay leaf
Salt and pepper
3 stalks celery, chopped
1 carrot, cut into pieces
½ onion, chopped

FOR THE SEAFOOD:
¾ cup extra virgin olive oil
1 large onion, chopped
3 bay leaves
3 cups chicken broth
2 shallots, minced
2 garlic cloves, minced
12 littleneck clams, scrubbed and drained
12 large mussels, scrubbed and drained
8 sea scallops
12 ounces cleaned calamari, bodies cut into rings, tentacles left
    whole
12 jumbo bay shrimp
3 sprigs fresh rosemary
3 sage leaves
1 teaspoon salt
1 teaspoon dried basil

½ teaspoon dried oregano
¼ teaspoon freshly ground black pepper
Red pepper flakes, to taste
2¼ cups arborio rice

To prepare the fish broth: Combine ingredients in medium pot. Let simmer for 30 minutes. Strain through cheesecloth.

To prepare the seafood: Heat ½ cup of the olive oil in a wide, 8–10 quart casserole over medium heat. Add onion and bay leaves and cook, stirring regularly until onions are golden brown—about 12 minutes. Pour the chicken broth into a small saucepan and warm on back burner.

Heat the remaining olive oil in a large Dutch oven. Add shallots and garlic and cook until lightly browned, about 5 minutes. Add clams, mussels, scallops, calamari, shrimp, rosemary, sage, salt, basil, oregano, and black and red pepper. Add fish broth, bring to a boil, and remove Dutch oven from the heat. Discard bay leaves.

When onions are golden brown in the casserole, add rice and stir well. Add the warm chicken broth a half cup at a time, stirring constantly with a wooden spoon until liquid is absorbed. Continue to cook at a gentle boil, stirring constantly, for about 5 minutes more. Add seafood and fish broth from the second pot and continue cooking, stirring constantly until rice is al dente, about 10 minutes. If rice gets too dry, add remaining broth as needed.

51.

Risotto ai Due Ghiottoni

Bari is a city not often frequented by American tourists (at least in comparison to Florence, Venice, Rome, Milan, etc.), but its distinctively Apulian cuisine deserves to be better known in this country. This very rich dish is a specialty of Ristorante ai Due Ghiottoni in Bari and is a creation of their chef Mario de Napoli. Mario cleverly substitutes cream, cheeses, and wine for some of the broth usually used in a risotto, with spectacular results. Again, a warning, this is very filling, so only light appetizers or salads ought to surround it.

MAKES: *4 servings* • PREPARATION TIME: *25 minutes* • DIFFICULTY: *3*

¼ pound frozen spinach, thawed and minced
2 cups chicken broth
¼ pound butter
½ onion, chopped
1 pound arborio rice
2 ounces prosciutto, diced
1 cup heavy cream

    1 cup white wine
    ¼ pound mozzarella cheese, diced
    ¼ pound Parmesan cheese, grated

Pour the chicken broth into a saucepan and warm on the back burner. Melt the butter in a medium skillet over medium heat and sauté the onion until translucent. Add the rice and prosciutto and mix with a wooden spoon until coated with butter. Add the warm broth a little at a time, stirring constantly. Once each addition is absorbed, add more. Add wine, then when all the liquids are absorbed, add cream, spinach, mozzarella, and Parmesan cheese. Mix all the ingredients thoroughly and serve.

52.

Polenta, Forester's Style
Polenta alla Boscaiola

Salvatore Caniglia and Tonino Mastellone are the co-owners of three of San Diego's finest Italian restaurants—the classy Buon Appetito and Sogno di Vino in Little Italy, and the more countrified I Trulli in Encinitas, San Diego county. Salvatore is from Taranto in Puglia and Tonino comes from Sorrento near Naples. Despite both chefs' southern Italian origins, this dish is more closely associated with northern Italy, especially the Lombard and Piedmont regions.

MAKES: *4 servings* • PREPARATION TIME: *½ hour* • DIFFICULTY: *3*

FOR THE POLENTA:
4 cups water
2 tablespoons olive oil
2 tablespoons grated Parmesan cheese
1 cup cornmeal (see note, p. 140)

(or 1 8-ounce tube pre-prepared polenta, cut into ½ inch slices)

For the Sauce:

3 tablespoons olive oil

1 pound mushrooms, mixed and sliced (porcini, shiitake, oyster, and crimini work well)

3 fresh garlic, cloves chopped

Salt and pepper

¾ cup white wine

3 ounces crumbled gorgonzola cheese

½ cup cream

½ cup chopped parsley

To prepare the polenta: Boil water over medium high heat in a medium non-stick saucepan and add olive oil. When water comes to a boil, add Parmesan cheese; then add all the cornmeal and stir with a wooden spoon making sure the polenta does not stick to the bottom of the pan. When the polenta thickens, pour onto a serving dish.

For a softer polenta, add a little more water while stirring. (Alternately, you can use the tube of pre-prepared polenta and sauté individual slices in olive oil until lightly browned.)

To prepare the sauce: Heat oil in a skillet over medium high heat and sauté the mushrooms for 3 minutes. Add garlic, and salt and pepper to taste and cook 4 minutes more. Add the wine, let reduce slightly; then add gorgonzola and cream and continue to cook for 4 minutes until sauce is a medium thick consistency. Turn off heat and sprinkle with parsley.

NOTE:

If making polenta from scratch, place a mound of polenta on each dish making a hole in the center so it looks like a volcano. Pour sauce into the hole and garnish with a sprig of parsley. If using store-bought polenta, buy an 8-ounce tube, cut into ½-inch slices, and arrange two slices on each of four plates and cover with sauce, also garnishing with parsley.

53.

Roasted Tomatoes and Polenta

The Gramercy Tavern on 20th Street has been New York's number one-rated restaurant for four of the last five years. Though it's not an Italian restaurant, Tom Collicho, the owner-chef is one of America's most innovative chefs and his own background is Italian. We asked him for a recipe that was connected to his Italian roots, and here's his response:

Everybody knows the best tomatoes come from New Jersey. When I was growing up in Elizabeth I thought countryside meant the suburbs until I was fourteen. We had a tomato vine growing in a small patch sowed between the fences of our backyard. Come late summer, there were more tomatoes than we knew what to do with.

My grandmother would make tomato puree that she would can in mason jars and use all winter long. But as I started to work in my own kitchens, I hit on another way to make the tomato harvest of late summer last longer: simply roast the tomatoes with a little garlic and thyme, which removes most of the water and intensifies the flavor. They freeze easily and can be used all winter. These roasted tomatoes are not as dehydrated as the sun-dried variety that seem to be everywhere (they also don't require reconstituting), and they perfectly illustrate the concept of starting with one "ingredient" and building outward, from simple to increasingly complex. The leftover roasted garlic, incidentally, has a creamy, mellow flavor not found in the raw vegetable and makes a great spread on a piece of crusty bread.

MAKES: *40 roasted tomato halves, about 20 roasted garlic cloves, and 1 to 3 cups roasted tomato juice* • PREPARATION TIME: *4 hours, 30 minutes* • DIFFICULTY: *3*

Special equipment: parchment paper (or aluminum foil); large, rimmed baking pans; and jars for storing tomatoes and garlic separately

For the Tomatoes:
20 ripe tomatoes, stems and cores removed
2 large heads garlic divided into unpeeled cloves
½ cup extra virgin olive oil
Kosher salt and freshly ground pepper
8 sprigs fresh thyme

For the Polenta:
1 cup cornmeal
4 cups water or vegetable broth
Kosher salt
¼ cup extra virgin olive oil
About ½ cup freshly grated Parmesan cheese

To prepare the tomatoes: Heat the oven to 350 degrees. Cut the tomatoes in half crosswise (through the equator), and then place the tomatoes, garlic, and olive oil in a large bowl. Season with salt and pepper to taste and mix gently. Line two large, rimmed baking sheets with parchment paper or aluminum foil. Place the tomato halves on the baking sheets, cut side down, and then pour any olive oil left in the bowl over them. Divide the garlic and thyme between the baking sheets and bake until the tomato skins loosen, about 20 minutes.

Remove and discard the tomato skins. Pour any juices that have accumulated into a bowl and reserve. Return the tomatoes to the oven and reduce the temperature to 275 degrees. Continue roasting, periodically pouring off and reserving the juices until the tomatoes are slightly shrunken and appear cooked and concentrated, but not yet dry, for about 3 to 4 hours more.

Remove the tomatoes from the oven and allow them to cool on the baking sheets. Discard the thyme and transfer the tomatoes and garlic to separate containers. Store the tomatoes, garlic, and reserved tomato juices in the refrigerator for up to 1 week or in the freezer for up to 6 months.

To prepare the polenta: In a bowl, moisten the cornmeal with 2 tablespoons of water, mixing well with your hands.

Bring 4 cups of water (or vegetable broth) to a boil in a medium saucepan over medium-high heat. Add a pinch of salt and gradually stir in the cornmeal. Stirring constantly with a wooden spoon, bring the polenta to a boil. Reduce the heat to low and cook the polenta, stirring occasionally, until it is no longer grainy, about 30 minutes. Stir in the olive oil and cheese, taste the polenta for salt, and remove it from the heat. Serve warm.

NOTE:

Serve tomatoes warm on a bed of polenta.

Meat and Poultry

In his classic study of Italian culinary traditions, The Food of Italy, *Waverly Root refers to a "meat line" that separates northern from southern Italy. Southern dishes, he notes, generally use less meat and more pasta, fish, and vegetables, all of which are relatively inexpensive and available locally. This is because historically the north has been more prosperous than the south, and meat simply costs more. These days the line is a bit more blurred and meat and poultry dishes are everywhere in Italy, but it is still the south where you will find more fish and vegetable dishes as main courses. Italian preparation of meat is generally quite simple—grilled or baked with a variety of herbs or sauces. Biba Caggiano's Broiled Cornish Game Hens in our collection is typical of those choices: spread the birds out flat, rub some salt and olive oil on them and put them on the grill until done.*

54.

Chicken Broccolatini

In 1969 Vincent Migliore opened a simple variety store in Somerville, Massachusetts. To satisfy his own desires, he added a small deli in the back, where he served tasty homemade eggplant and meatball sandwiches. As its popularity grew, Vinny slowly expanded the food business. In 1986, he opened a restaurant in the back that at first served only lunch. In 1995, due to overwhelming demand, he finally opened in the evening for dinner; hence, the striking name, Vinny's at Night. The restaurant has been recognized as one of the best Italian restaurants in Boston by all the major publications, and we're delighted to offer you one of Vinny's favorite recipes.

MAKES: *4 servings* • PREPARATION TIME: *40 minutes* • DIFFICULTY: *2*

Special equipment: meat mallet (see p. 4) and kitchen twine

Preheat oven to 500 degrees.

For the Chicken:
4 chicken breasts, skinned and boned
Fresh basil, chopped
Fresh parsley, chopped, to taste
Olive oil
Parmesan cheese, grated
Salt and pepper
8 thin slices of prosciutto
½ cup sun-dried tomatoes
8 slices Swiss cheese

For the Broccolatini:
1 28-ounce jar premium marinara sauce
1 14-ounce can chicken broth

To prepare the chicken: Butterfly chicken breasts and place them on a hard surface. Cover them with plastic wrap and flatten with a meat mallet, without breaking them apart. Once breasts are nice and flat, do not move them. Season breasts with basil, parsley, oil, Parmesan cheese, salt, and pepper. Place two slices of prosciutto on each breast and sprinkle sun-dried tomatoes on top of prosciutto. Then add Swiss cheese to cover tomatoes and prosciutto.

To assemble the broccolatini: Preheat oven to 500 degrees. Take some spinach (as much as you want) and roll the breasts up tightly. Tie each rolled breast securely with at least two pieces of twine. Heat olive oil in a large sauté pan, place the *broccolatini* in pan, and cook them uniformly until they are nice and brown. Pour sauce and broth into baking pan, mix, add the *broccolatini,* and bake them for about 20 minutes or until sauce is boiling. Serve piping hot.

55.

Biba Caggiano's Broiled Cornish Game Hens

Biba Caggiano is an author, teacher, and restaurateur. Biba, her restaurant in Sacramento, California, is a must stop for anyone in the area who loves Italian food.

This simple but unique recipe for Cornish game hens is a splendid meal for any occasion—and the presentation makes it visually stimulating for company as well.

You can serve this with a side dish of sautéed small white onions or roasted potatoes.

MAKES: *4 servings* • PREPARATION TIME: *45 minutes* • DIFFICULTY: *2*

Special equipment: meat mallet (see p. 4)

Preheat broiler or prepare barbeque.

4 Cornish game hens
⅓ cup extra virgin olive oil
Salt and freshly ground pepper

Lemon wedges
Parsley, for garnish

Cut Cornish hens lengthwise along entire backbone. Split hens open and place skin side down on a cutting board. With a meat mallet or the flat side of a large cleaver, flatten hens, taking care not to break the bones. Wash and dry thoroughly.

Combine oil, salt, and plenty of pepper in a small bowl. Brush hens on both sides with oil mixture. Place in a large, shallow dish and pour remaining oil over hens. Let stand at room temperature for about 2 hours, basting several times with oil mixture.

Preheat broiler or prepare barbecue. Arrange hens skin side facing heat. Cook 10 to 15 minutes, being careful not to burn skin. Turn a few times and baste with oil mixture. Cook 10 to 15 minutes longer or until tender. Season with additional pepper. Place on a warm platter. Garnish with lemon wedges and parsley. Serve immediately.

56.

Raspberry Chicken
Pollo ai Lamponi

"Food and Wine at its Prime" is the mantra of Orlando Andreani, owner of San Marco Ristorante, specializing in northern Italian cuisine and located in Hauppauge, New York. For over twenty years, Andreani, along with Chef/ Partner Jose Rodrigues, has delighted the taste buds of Long Islanders longing for classic Italian cooking that you only used to be able to get inside the Five Boroughs of New York City.

Here they share one of their outstanding main courses—one that adds raspberry to its sauce to give it an extra zing.

MAKES: *4 servings* • PREPARATION TIME: *30 minutes* • DIFFICULTY: *2*

Special equipment: Meat mallet (see p. 4)

FOR THE CHICKEN:
8 chicken breast halves (about 3 ounces each)
1 cup all-purpose flour

3 medium eggs, lightly beaten
1 cup olive oil (not virgin)
Salt and pepper

For the Sauce:
1 cup red wine vinegar
5 ounces extra fine sugar
1 cup prepared brown sauce or gravy—you can use powdered
  brown gravy mix and prepare according to packaged directions
½ quart raspberry preserves

To prepare the chicken: Place chicken breasts on hard surface. Cover them with plastic wrap and flatten with a meat mallet to ¼-inch thickness. Once breasts are flat, dip chicken breasts in flour on both sides, shake off excess, then dip in eggs. In a large skillet, heat the oil, add the coated chicken, and sauté for 3 minutes each side. Don't crowd the chicken in the skillet—do this in 2 or 3 batches if necessary. Add salt and pepper to taste. Remove breasts from skillet and save on a platter lined with paper towels.

To prepare the sauce: Discard oil from skillet and add the vinegar and sugar to same pan. Cook for about 10 minutes at low heat, stirring frequently. Add raspberry preserves and brown gravy, cook for 5 minutes at low heat, stirring frequently.

Add chicken breasts to the skillet 3 or 4 at a time and cook for another 10 minutes, spooning the sauce on top several times. Transfer to serving platter and garnish with fresh raspberry.

NOTE:

For extra pizazz, add a little raspberry wine to the sauce while the chicken is cooking.

57.

Hunter's Chicken
Chicken Cacciatore

According to food historian Linda Stradley, chicken cacciatore originated in central Italy during the Renaissance, when only the upper class could hunt for sport and therefore were the only ones privileged enough to enjoy this meal.

This dish is popular and easy. This version uses boneless, skinless chicken breasts, which makes it low in fat as well. Once all the preparation is done, it's just a matter of letting the chicken stew in its juices, creating a flavorful and classic Italian main course.

MAKES: *4 servings* • PREPARATION TIME: *1 hour, 30 minutes* • DIFFICULTY: *2*

3 pounds boneless, skinless chicken breasts
¼ cup olive oil
½ cup chopped onion
1 pound fresh tomatoes chopped in small pieces, or a 28-ounce
    can of tomato sauce (makes a smoother sauce)
8 ounces sliced mushrooms
½ cup dry white wine

1 teaspoon salt
¼ teaspoon pepper
½ bay leaf
⅛ teaspoon fresh thyme leaves
¼ teaspoon fresh marjoram

Tear each of the chicken breasts into 2 or 3 thinner fillets. Heat oil in large skillet over medium heat and sauté in oil until golden brown. Drain. Combine remaining ingredients in a large pot. Add chicken. Cover and simmer slowly, stirring occasionally. (The longer the better. One hour is optimum, but a half hour will do.)

NOTE:

Serve a couple of the smaller pieces of chicken with a healthy dollop of skillet mushrooms and sauce over rice, or serve the chicken with rice on the side. Goes great with green beans or broccoli.

58.
Chicken Scarpiella

This recipe comes from Magnifico Restaurant in the Chelsea section of Manhattan. The Magnifico family comes from Ischia, a little island near Capri, off the coast of Naples. Alfredo, the owner of Magnifico's, dictated the recipe to us on the spot when we dined there recently. This is a very popular dish in restaurants on Long Island and is sometimes known as Chicken Scarpata, but it's hard to find outside of New York. It's easy to make, and the mix of sausages and chicken creates a sublime pork-poultry flavor that is distinctive and uncommon.

MAKES: *4 servings* • PREPARATION TIME: *25 minutes* • DIFFICULTY: *2*

½ cup extra-virgin olive oil
5 garlic cloves, peeled and sliced
4 chicken thighs, boned, skinned, and chopped in quarters
4 chicken breasts, boned, skinned, and chopped in quarters
4 links of mild (or hot, if you want extra spiciness) Italian sausage
All-purpose flour

2 tablespoons chopped rosemary
1 cup dry white wine (Chardonnay or Pinot Grigio is fine)
Juice from 1 lemon
1 14-ounce can chicken broth

Heat olive oil in a large skillet over medium-low heat and sauté sliced garlic until just lightly brown. (Do not overcook or the garlic will become bitter.) Dredge chicken and sausage in flour and add to skillet. Cook for about 10–12 minutes, turning once and sprinkling both sides with rosemary as you turn. Add wine and continue cooking until wine is reduced to about half. Squeeze lemon juice over all. (If the meat seems too dry, add chicken stock.) Remove chicken and sausage from skillet, place on platter and pour the remaining sauce (scraping up the bits and pieces) over the meat.

NOTE:

Serve with pasta, mashed potatoes, or rice.

59.
Chicken Parmesan

Chicken Parmesan is a member of the "dip and cook" type of Italian food. This dish is very versatile. You can serve it with a side dish of sliced shiitake mushrooms sautéed in butter and basil, or top it with mozzarella and tomato sauce and serve with a side dish of your favorite pasta. It's also good with a béchamel (see p. 81) sauce or with a twist of lemon juice. Chicken Parmesan is a standard in the Italian food canon, one that every Italian cook should know.

MAKES: *4 servings* • PREPARATION TIME: *25 minutes* • DIFFICULTY: *2*

Special equipment: meat mallet (p. 4)

4 chicken breast halves, skinned and boned
¾ cup all-purpose flour
2 large eggs
1 cup bread crumbs
½ cup freshly grated Parmesan cheese

3 tablespoons fresh parsley, chopped fine
⅓ cup extra virgin olive oil
Salt and freshly ground pepper

Trim fat from chicken breasts and cut out the tendon from the fillet. Place breasts on a large sheet of waxed paper and cover with another sheet of the same size. Pound cutlets with meat mallet until they are quite thin—¼ inch or less. Coat pounded cutlets with flour (dredge through flour on both sides) and shake off excess. Place eggs in wide bowl and beat until yolks and whites are well mixed. Put bread crumbs, cheese, and parsley on a flat plate and mix. Dip each floured cutlet first into egg and then into crumb mixture. Set cutlets on wire rack for 15 minutes or so until coating coheres.

Heat oil in large skillet over medium-high heat, and fry cutlets two at a time until coating on one side is crisp and golden brown. Turn cutlets over and brown the other side for about 2 minutes. Drain on paper towels and repeat with remaining cutlets. Sprinkle with salt and pepper and serve immediately.

VARIATION: Place cutlets on baking sheet and cover each with a large slice of whole milk mozzarella. Remove from oven when cheese has melted and top with your favorite heated tomato sauce.

60.

Italian Skillet

Many of the recipes in this book have been handed down from generation to generation through an Italian family. When Sandy Maggiore left the family nest, her mother had a gift for her: a handwritten cookbook she had painstakingly created and filled with the family's best recipes. It's a gift Sandy still treasures, and we were lucky enough to have had a peek inside. This is one of the easier recipes, a cheesy, juicy "skillet" of Italian flavors.

MAKES: *4 servings* • PREPARATION TIME: *20 minutes* • DIFFICULTY: *2*

2 tablespoons olive oil
¾ pound lean ground beef
Salt and pepper
1 15-ounce can or jar prepared tomato sauce
¼ tablespoon fresh oregano, chopped
2 cups cooked arborio rice (see cooking directions on p. 26) (use
   less than 1 cup raw)
½ pound whole milk mozzarella

Heat oil in medium skillet over medium heat and brown beef; pour off fat when done. Sprinkle beef with salt and pepper. Add tomato sauce, oregano, and rice. Toss. Cover and simmer for five minutes. Cut cheese in round slices and place on top of mixture, covering completely. Cover skillet and continue heating until cheese melts. Serve hot and gooey.

61.

Drunken Pork Loin

Grandfather Stephen Moramarco used to make a version of this, and though we never got a recipe from him, this is probably a fairly accurate reconstruction. The loin is cooked in wine and then covered with wine sauce, so the name of the dish is certainly appropriate. Don't serve this to anyone who has a problem with alcohol; for them you might want to substitute Pork Shoulder in Milk (see p. 165) instead.

MAKES: *4 servings* • PREPARATION TIME: *30 minutes* • DIFFICULTY: *2*

FOR THE PORK:
2 pounds pork loin, lean and boneless
Salt and pepper
3 tablespoons extra-virgin olive oil
1 garlic clove, minced
¾ cup Chianti wine
1½ tablespoons chopped parsley

For the Wine Sauce:

2 tablespoons extra virgin olive oil

¼ sweet onion, minced

½ green pepper, chopped into small pieces

1 cup tomato sauce (canned, or Fresh Tomato Sauce, see p. 77)

¼ cup red wine

1 teaspoon red pepper flakes (optional)

To prepare the pork: Season pork loin well with salt and pepper, rubbing it liberally over the surface. Heat olive oil and garlic in large skillet over medium heat, and when oil is hot, add seasoned loin and brown on all sides. Add wine and parsley, turn heat to low, and simmer until pork is cooked through, about 20 to 30 minutes.

To prepare the wine sauce: Heat olive oil in medium skillet, and add onions and pepper. When onions are translucent, add tomato sauce and wine. Sprinkle with red pepper flakes if using.

When pork is done, transfer to hot platter and cover with wine sauce. Pass additional sauce separately.

62.

Pork Shoulder in Milk

Grandmother Vivian Codiga (whose surname is Rinaldi) created this gem, which can be found in her family's cookbook. Italians are known for their inventiveness in the kitchen, and this entrée was simply inspired by the ingredients (or lack thereof) on hand. Vivian's son, Paul, remembers that his grandfather was so impatient to eat this dish before it cooled that he would always burn his mouth. This recipe may take a while, but once you taste the pork slices smothered in the milky sauce, you will realize it was worth the wait.

MAKES: *4 servings* • PREPARATION TIME: *2 hours* • DIFFICULTY: *4*

4 pounds pork butt or shoulders
Sea salt and freshly ground pepper
1 medium lemon, washed
8 tablespoons olive oil
8 tablespoons unsalted butter
4 quarts whole milk

Generously season the pork with salt and pepper on all sides. Zest the whole lemon and reserve the zest; then slice the lemon in half. Squeeze the juice from one half of the lemon into a small bowl; reserve the remaining half. Heat the olive oil and butter in a heavy-bottomed Dutch oven, just large enough to hold the pork pieces. When melted, add the pork. Lightly brown the meat on all sides, adjusting heat as necessary. With the pork still in the Dutch oven, add the milk. It will boil almost immediately. Reduce the heat to a gentle simmer; add the zest and lemon juice. Cover the Dutch oven.

Check periodically to see that the Dutch oven is not drying out; add more milk if it gets below three quarters of the pork. The pork will take at least two hours to become tender. When the pork is fork tender and cooked, the milk will have curdled into brown nuggets. Carefully remove the meat and set aside. Place a strainer or fine colander over a bowl or saucepan large enough to contain the pork's broth. Carefully pour the broth through the strainer (it's hot and can burn); the sieve will collect the curdled milk. Return the curds to the Dutch oven.

The pork will have rendered a great deal of fat, so the broth must be degreased before you make the sauce. Skim the fat off the surface with a large spoon; then return the degreased broth to the Dutch oven with the curds. Squeeze the juice from the remaining lemon half into the Dutch oven. Transfer to a blender or food processor and puree the sauce until smooth. Season with salt and pepper to taste. Slice the meat and spoon sauce over top.

NOTE:

Serve with a very soft polenta flavored with Parmesan cheese (see p. 138).

63.

Osso Buco

A tender piece of veal is a staple of the northern Italian diet. This dish originated in Milan; the name osso buco literally means "bone hole," referring to the large veal shank bone filled with marrow. A well-cooked veal shank is simmered for a long while so that the meat barely clings to the bone. It's a good idea to use "organic" veal, which means the veal calves were humanely treated so that you'll have less guilt while enjoying this classic Milanese dish. This recipe comes from Aurora Trattoria in La Jolla, California.

MAKES: *4 servings* • PREPARATION TIME: *1 hour, 30 minutes* • DIFFICULTY: *3*

½ cup of vegetable oil
½ cup of flour
4 veal shanks
1 large onion
Peel of 1 lemon, chopped
4 bay leaves
2 tablespoons olive oil

½ bottle Pinot Grigio
24 ounces of whole tomatos in puree, do not drain
2 medium carrots, chopped
3 stalks of celery, chopped
1 teaspoon rosemary
1 teaspoon sage
⅛ teaspoon salt
⅛ teaspoon white pepper

Heat vegetable oil in large skillet over medium heat. Flour the shanks, and shake off excess flour. When oil is hot, place the shanks in skillet to brown on all sides. Discard the oil. In same pan, heat olive oil and sauté the onions, lemon peel, and bay leaves. When the vegetable mixture is cooked but not too brown, add white wine and reduce by half. Add tomatoes, carrots, celery, rosemary, oregano, salt, white pepper, and add veal shanks, and bring to a boil. Reduce heat and simmer until tender, about one hour.

Remove shanks from the pan, and sift the sauce through a food mill (or blend in food processor and strain through a strainer). Put the shanks and sauce together.

NOTE:

Osso buco goes well with Risotto Milanese (see p. 131), pasta, or mashed potatoes. Pour the delicious sauce over everything.

64.
My Father's Braciole

Federico recalls: "One of the small treasures my father, Stephen (for whom my son and co-author is named), passed on to me was a sauce-stained index card with a recipe for his version of *braciole,* the herbed beef rolls he made, usually served in tomato sauce. Somehow over the years this index card was lost, but I made the dish so many times that it became second nature. Pronounced brah-*zhol*-le, the word literally means 'chops,' but in this recipe it refers to a braised beef roll, which is sometimes called *brasato.* These beef delights are a completely Italian way to cook beef—always tender, flavorful, and rich."

MAKES: *6 servings* • PREPARATION TIME: *1 hour, 30 minutes* • DIFFICULTY: *3*

Special equipment: meat mallet (see p. 4); heavy kitchen twine

6 thinly sliced round or cube steaks
¼ cup extra-virgin olive oil
2 tablespoons chopped, fresh parsley

1 tablespoon chopped, fresh oregano
3 large garlic cloves, minced
6 slices prosciutto (or bacon)
¼ pound pecorino cheese, grated
1 28-ounce jar premium tomato sauce.
Salt and pepper

Flatten each beef slice with meat mallet to about ¼-inch thickness. Coat both sides of meat with a layer of olive oil. Sprinkle each slice with parsley, oregano, and minced garlic. Top with a slice of prociutto and grated cheese. Roll up each slice and tie beef roll with heavy twine. Heat skillet coated with olive oil and brown beef roll on all sides. Add tomato sauce and salt and pepper to taste, and simmer for one hour. Remove *braciola* from sauce and cut twine.

NOTE:

Serve with pasta.

65

Braciole, Sicilian-Style

Farsumagru

The "Little Italy" of St. Louis, Missouri, is located in an area commonly known as the Hill. The Italians nicknamed it *La Montagna* (The Mountain) because of its steep incline, which they had to walk up every day to return home after a hard day of labor in the local clay and coal mines.

The Gitto family has a long proud history on the Hill; they own a restaurant called On the Hill, which offers a wide variety of Italian and fusion dishes and is one of the city's best-loved establishments. We're just delighted that Anna Gitto shared this family recipe with us.

The word *farsumagru* means "false lean," which may refer to the fact that it is made with round steak, which has very little fat, but when you add salami and hard-boiled eggs to it, that outside "lean" look is false indeed.

MAKES: *4 servings* • PREPARATION TIME: *1 hour, 45 minutes* • DIFFICULTY: *3*

Special equipment: meat mallet (see p. 4); kitchen twine

For the Braciole:
1 pound round steak
Salt and pepper
Garlic, granulated
1 cup packaged seasoned bread crumbs
½ pound sliced salami
3 hard-boiled eggs, cut in half lengthwise or sliced in an egg slicer
1 cup finely chopped onions or scallions
½ cup shaved Parmesan cheese
3 tablespoons extra virgin olive oil

Fresh Tomato Sauce (see p. 77) or your favorite pasta sauce
1 cup canned tomatoes, crushed

To assemble the braciole: Lay the round steak flat and pound to a ¼-inch thickness with a meat mallet (you can also ask your butcher to tenderize it for you). Season with salt, pepper, and garlic to taste. Sprinkle on seasoned bread crumbs; then layer salami covering the entire surface. Layer the hard-boiled egg slices over the salami, and sprinkle with chopped onions or scallions. (Leave about an inch along the edges of the steak when layering the ingredients.) Sprinkle cheese as last layer, roll steak tightly, and tie with twine in at least 3 or 4 places.

Heat oil in large skillet over medium heat and brown rolled steak on all sides. After browning, add the steak roll to your favorite pasta sauce and let it simmer over very low heat for at least 1 hour or more in the sauce. Turn roll several times while simmering. During last ten minutes, simmer crushed tomatoes in a separate pan until warm and bubbling. Remove the steak roll from the sauce, and cut the roll into slices. Arrange slices on a platter and pour a little of the sauce over the roll. Top with crushed tomatoes and serve.

66.

Pan-Roasted Lamb Loin with Black Olives

Agnello alle Olive Nere

Antonio Tommasi the owner-chef of Ca' Brea, an exquisite Italian eatery in the heart of Los Angeles. Antonio comes from the Veneto region and has written his own book entitled *Italy Anywhere,** where this recipe originally appeared. Once the ingredients are prepared, it takes just over 5 minutes to cook. The lamb makes a thick, savory sauce that goes well with *peperonata*, a sweet pepper side dish, for an interesting contrast of flavors.

MAKES: *4 servings* • PREPARATION TIME: *30 minutes* • DIFFICULTY: *2*

  3 cloves garlic, crushed
  3 tablespoons extra virgin olive oil
  ⅓ cup diced Italian pancetta (bacon)
  4 to 5 sprigs of fresh thyme
  1 small sprig of rosemary

---

*Lori De Mori, Jean-Louis De Mori, and Antonio Tommasi, *Italy Anywhere: Living an Italian Culinary Life Wherever You Call Home* (New York: Viking, 2000).

1 teaspoon capers
1½ pounds lamb loin, trimmed and cut into chunks
Freshly ground pepper
1 cup Italian or Spanish black olives, pits removed
2 tablespoons dry white wine
2 medium very ripe tomatoes, peeled (see note), seeded, and
    crushed
Salt

Warm the garlic and oil in a large, heavy-bottomed pan over medium heat. When the garlic begins to color, add the pancetta, thyme, and rosemary, stir for a couple of minutes, and then sprinkle in the capers. Stir the ingredients well; then add in the lamb chunks and a generous grinding of pepper. Sauté for 2 minutes; stir in the olives.

When the meat has browned lightly on all sides, add the wine and stir well while the wine reduces. Add the tomatoes, simmer gently for a couple of minutes, add salt to taste, and serve.

NOTE:

Put washed tomatoes in boiling water for 1 minute or less, plunge in bowl of ice water until cool enough to handle, and then peel.

67.

Grilled Lamb Chops with Sautéed Vegetables

This recipe comes from Antonio Petrone, chef at Cicolella in Fiera, a restaurant in Foggia, Italy. On a visit to Apulia one summer, we stopped for a night in Foggia and had dinner at Antonio's restaurant. While we were there, an Italian wedding was in full swing with a sit-down meal for over one hundred guests. It was already late in the evening when we arrived, but apparently the wedding and the feast had been going on since midmorning. We sat and chatted, lingering over this succulent dish, and when we retired for the day, the wedding was still going strong and showed no signs of slowing, in typical Italian fashion.

MAKES: *4 servings* • PREPARATION TIME: *30 minutes* • DIFFICULTY: *2*

Special equipment: barbecue grill and coal

8 loin lamb chops
¼ cup extra-virgin olive oil
1 large onion, thinly sliced

¼ pound Italian or crimini mushrooms, sliced
2 zucchini, peeled, quartered, and halved
2 red bell peppers, sliced into strips
4 plum tomatoes, quartered
¼ cup dry white wine
2 tablespoons Italian parsley, chopped
Salt and pepper
Parmesan cheese, grated

Prepare barbecue grill with hot coals. (It can also be prepared on an indoor grill.) When charcoal is white hot, grill chops for 4–5 minutes per side, being careful not to burn. Remove the chops from the grill and set aside. Heat olive oil in a large skillet. Sauté the onion over medium heat until translucent. Add the mushrooms and zucchini and sauté for 3 minutes. Add bell peppers and sauté for 2 more minutes. Add tomatoes and sauté for 2 minutes, and then toss all vegetables vigorously. Add wine and lamb chops to vegetable mixture and simmer over low heat until wine evaporates and lamb chops are heated through. Divide the chops and vegetables among four plates, sprinkle with Parmesan cheese, salt, and pepper, all to taste, and chopped parsley. Serve immediately.

68.

Veal alla "Ecco"

Here's a creamy, buttery take on a veal dish, courtesy of Campagnola Restaurant on New York's Upper East Side. For over twenty years, owner-chef Etienne Lizzi has been serving southern Italian food to the raves of neighbors and visitors alike. This elegant entrée is a robust treat, perfect for unexpected company, as it can be made very quickly and easily at the last minute.

MAKES: *4 servings* • PREPARATION TIME: *30 minutes* • DIFFICULTY LEVEL: *2*

1½ pounds loin of veal
Salt and pepper
1 tablespoon all-purpose flour
2 ounces olive oil
2 ounces white wine
2 cups heavy cream
Juice from 1 medium lemon
4 ounces butter

12 medium pieces artichoke hearts (boiled until soft if fresh, but
   easier if canned or frozen)
1 cup grated Parmesan cheese
1 tablespoon parsley

Slice the veal in 12 ½-inch scallops (small thin slices) and season with salt and pepper to taste. Dust both sides with flour. Heat olive oil in a medium oven-proof skillet over medium heat and sauté on both sides for 1 minute. Add wine, heavy cream, lemon juice, and butter, and let simmer for 5 minutes. Do not overcook. Finally, place the scallops under the broiler for another minute to get a nice golden brown topping.

After scallops have been removed from boiler, place artichokes in center of plate. Remove scallops from skillet and place around artichokes. Top with cheese and sprinkled parsley.

69.
Veal Piccata

Veal Piccata is a well-known Italian recipe that's both simple and quick. Essentially, it's a thin slice of veal, dusted with flour, and cooked with some lemon, wine, and garlic. The minimal ingredients serve to accent the veal's innately delicate flavors without overpowering them. If you are making a dinner, be sure that this is the last thing you put on the stove, as it cooks rather quickly, and it is best served fresh from the pan. And be sure, as in Veal alla "Ecco" (see 178), not to overcook the veal because it gets tough when overdone.

MAKES: *4 servings* • PREPARATION TIME: *10 minutes or less* • DIFFICULTY: *1*

Special equipment: meat mallet (see p. 4)

4 boneless veal scallops
½ cup all-purpose unbleached flour
Salt and pepper
2 tablespoons olive oil

Juice from 1 medium lemon
¼ cup dry white wine
1 tablespoon fresh minced garlic
¼ cup chicken broth
2 tablespoons butter
1 tablespoon chopped fresh Italian parsley

Place veal scallops between 2 pieces of plastic wrap and pound to about ¼ inch thick with a meat mallet. Dip veal scallops in flour on both sides, and sprinkle with salt and pepper. Heat oil in medium skillet over high heat. Sauté scallops on each side for approximately 1 minute until lightly brown. Remove from heat and set aside. Turn heat to medium, add lemon, wine, garlic, stock, and butter, and let simmer for a couple of minutes, removing any burnt flour bits. Return veal to pan to cook for another minute on each side. Remove from heat and serve immediately, topping each veal scallop with pan sauce and garnishing with parsley.

70.

Veal alla "Diana"

It's truly a family affair at Frank Papa's Ristorante, located in St. Louis, Missouri. When Frank Papa isn't in the kitchen, his nephew Rob takes over. The restaurant first opened in 1994 with seventeen tables in one room. After five years in business, they expanded, adding a full bar area and a dine-in wine cellar. Now they can accommodate 150 people, a sure sign of success. Here is their popular veal entrée, named after Frank's wife, who is co-owner of the restaurant. It's based on a traditional Veal Piccata (see p. 180), but a little richer.

MAKES: *4 servings* • PREPARATION TIME: *15 minutes* • DIFFICULTY: *2*

    4 ounces clarified butter (see note, p. 124)
    2 tablespoons all-purpose flour, spread on plate
    1½ pounds veal scallopini, pounded thin
    2 cups sliced mushrooms
    2 tablespoons chopped fresh tomato
    1 teaspoon garlic

4 ounces sherry wine
12 ounces beef broth
2 tablespoons chopped fresh basil
4 tablespoons unsalted creamy butter, room temperature
Salt and pepper

Heat half of the clarified butter in skillet until hot. Flour veal, shake excess, and sauté over medium-high heat for just two or three minutes per side. Remove veal from skillet and set aside. Lower heat to medium, add remaining clarified butter and sauté mushrooms, then the tomatoes, and garlic. Toss until all are tender and the garlic is not yet brown. Add sherry and reduce by half. Add broth and basil, and reduce by one-third. Mix the butter and flour, add to sauce and whisk. Return veal to skillet, swirl in sauce, and season with salt and pepper to taste. Serve immediately.

NOTE:

This is great with rice or minimally dressed pasta.

71.

Cotecchino with Lentils, Bacon, and Truffle Oil

In northern Italy, it's customary to eat lentils and cotecchino (a wide Italian pork sausage) on December 31 for prosperity in the New Year. Tradition has it that the lentils symbolize money and the sausage signifies luck.

Zazu, a gourmet Italian restaurant in Santa Rosa, California, has created an elegant variation so full of rich ingredients that's it's almost like making and breaking all your New Year's resolutions at once. You can get a close approximation by using your favorite store-bought sausage, pancetta, or bacon and foregoing the truffle oil if necessary. But if you can find cotecchino in your area, use that.

MAKES: *6 servings* • PREPARATION TIME: *1 hour (or more)* • DIFFICULTY: *3*

¼ cup olive oil
⅓ pound quality pancetta or bacon, finely chopped
1 onion, diced small
1 medium carrot, peeled and diced small
1 celery rib, diced small

2 garlic cloves, minced
1 teaspoon chili flakes
1 pound sausage (see note below)
1 pound lentils
1 medium head green cabbage, sliced in wide strips
8 cups chicken stock (see appendix E) or canned broth
4 fresh bay leaves
1 teaspoon truffle oil (optional)
Salt and freshly ground pepper

Heat olive oil in a large pot on medium-high heat, sauté the bacon, onion, carrots, and celery, until fragrant and beginning to brown (about 5 minutes). Add the garlic and chili flakes and sauté another minute. Prick the sausages with a fork. Add the sausages, lentils, cabbage, stock, and bay leaves and bring to a boil. Do not add salt to cooking lentils! Reduce the heat to a low simmer. Cook until lentils and sausage are done, about 30 minutes. Add truffle oil if using, mix and season with salt and pepper to taste.

NOTE:

If you do use real cotecchino, you will have to cook them separately on low heat, as it takes them 1½–2 hours to cook.

Seafood

FRUTTI DI MARE

Because Italy is a peninsula and parts of it (Sicily and Sardenia) are islands, it's natural that seafood is an important and central part of the Italian diet. In most large cities in America, there are entire restaurants devoted to Italian seafood preparations, and in Italy, of course, you'll find them everywhere. Italians love the frutti di mare—the fruits of the sea—and the Adriatic remains a prime source of edible seafood for the entire region. All along the Adriatic coast and Sicily are fishing villages and fresh seafood markets, which to this day provide an abundance for the Italian table. Although many of the varieties of fish served in Italy are not found in U.S. waters, and though we can often substitute an equivalent fish type, the resulting product is not quite like the Italian original. But scallops, salmon, and shellfish are everywhere, so we've focused—except for the Cioppino, which calls for different kinds of fish—on those varieties.

72.

Seared Sea Scallops on a Potato and Chive Cake with White Truffles

Try this recipe when you're in a decadent mood—it's complex, but worth it. It comes from Lusardi's, one of New York's finest family-run restaurants.

This dish calls for the delectable and expensive white truffle (see *Italian Pride,** Reason 99). Chef Claudio Meneghini notes that you may substitute black or summer truffles when white truffles are not in season "or very pricey." But you might want to splurge just this once to see what the fuss is all about. This recipe should be attempted by advanced chefs only or those with patience and a sense of adventure.

MAKES: *4 servings* • PREPARATION TIME: *2 hours* • DIFFICULTY: *5*

FOR THE POTATO AND CHIVE CAKE:
2 medium-sized Idaho potatoes
1 egg yolk
4 tablespoons grated Parmesan cheese

*Citadel Press, 2000.

1 tablespoon white truffle oil
20 chives, chopped
Salt and pepper
4 tablespoons extra virgin olive oil

FOR THE WHITE TRUFFLE BUTTER:
2 tablespoons unsalted butter (softened)
1 tablespoon grated Parmesan cheese
1 tablespoon white truffle oil
1 medium-sized white truffle

FOR THE SCALLOPS:
12 large dry sea scallops (request size U10 from your fishmonger)
½ teaspoon salt
¼ teaspoon white pepper
1 tablespoon all-purpose flour
4 tablespoons extra virgin olive oil
½ cup medium dry white wine
1 cup heavy cream
1 tablespoon white truffle butter
4 potato and chive cakes (prepared separately, but seared at this step)

To prepare the potato and chive cake: Put potatoes in pot of cold water. Heat until boiling. Boil the potatoes (skin on) for 20 minutes. Cook until fork tender and drain. When potatoes are warm, peel and mash. Add the egg yolk, cheese, truffle oil, chives, and salt and pepper to taste. Mix all the ingredients by hand, obtaining a soft, but consistent, dough. Then divide it into 4 equal parts. Using the palms of your hands, form a ball out of each part and press down giving it a patty shape. Refrigerate for 1 hour.

To prepare the truffle butter: When the potato cakes have been in the refrigerator for 30 minutes, start to prepare the truffle butter.

In a cup, mix the softened butter with the cheese and truffle oil. Peel the white truffle, chop the peelings, add them to the butter mixture and refrigerate for about an hour. Reserve the remaining white truffle to be shaved as garnish.

To prepare the scallops: Start the scallops after you refrigerate the truffle butter. Wash the scallops very well and dry them with a kitchen towel. Arrange them on a plate, season with salt and white pepper, and dust them with the flour. Heat oil a large nonstick skillet over medium heat and allow it to warm. Add the scallops and brown them on both sides. Pour in the wine and allow it to evaporate by two-thirds; then add the cream and truffle butter, and reduce. While the sauce is reducing, remove potato cakes from refrigerator. Heat the remaining oil in a separate nonstick pan and sear the potato cakes.

NOTE:

Warm 4 plates. Place a potato cake in the center of each plate. Arrange 3 scallops on top of every potato cake, and divide the sauce equally. Garnish with white truffle shavings and serve.

74.

Sautéed Sea Scallops with Eggplant and Porcini Mushrooms

Hosteria Mazzei is the first restaurant in Westchester County, New York, to specialize in food from Apulia. (For more information on Apulia, please see *Italian Pride*, Reason 31.) Here is a recipe that marries three distinctive flavors and textures: the silkiness of scallops, the chewiness of eggplant, and the smell of pungent porcini mushrooms to create an unusual and original dish.

MAKES: *4 servings* • PREPARATION TIME: *30 minutes* • DIFFICULTY: *3*

Salt
1 small eggplant, peeled and cut into 4 thick slices
¼ cup all-purpose flour, spread on plate
1 egg, beaten with a pinch of salt
⅓ cup bread crumbs
½ cup extra virgin olive oil, divided
8 fresh sea scallops
1 clove garlic, chopped
5 basil leaves, chopped

4 plum tomatoes, peeled (see note, p. 175), seeded, and roughly
  chopped
Salt and pepper
4 fresh porcini mushrooms, cleaned and julienned

Salt the eggplant slices and let drain in colander for about 10 minutes to remove bitterness. Dredge slices in the flour and shake off excess. Dip into the
egg mixture and then into the bread crumbs, coating well. Warm 3 tablespoons of the oil in a skillet over medium heat and sauté the eggplant slices
until golden brown and tender. Drain on paper towels and set aside.

Slice scallops in half horizontally to make two thin disks. Warm two tablespoons of the olive oil in another skillet over medium-high heat. Add the garlic, basil, and scallops, and sauté until the scallops are cooked through, about
2 to 3 minutes. Turn the scallops once during cooking.

Place the tomatoes in a blender along with the remaining olive oil, salt, and
pepper, and puree until smooth. Transfer to small saucepan and cook over
medium heat, stirring regularly until the puree is heated through. (About 5
minutes.) Place 1 slice of eggplant in the center of each plate. Top each with
some scallops and porcini mushrooms. Spoon some of the tomato emulsion
around plate and serve.

74.

Cioppino

Cioppino is a hearty fish stew created by Sicilian fishermen living in San Francisco to help them get through their long days and nights at sea. The warm broth and hearty chunks of fresh seafood helped ward off colds and increased morale. Although the Sicilians living and working at Fisherman's Wharf are but a memory, their legacy and love of the sea lives on in this soup.

The Stinking Rose, a garlic-themed restaurant located in San Francisco's North Beach and Los Angeles contributed this recipe from its cookbook, *The Stinking Cookbook,* * a must for garlic lovers everywhere.

MAKES: *6–8 servings* • PREPARATION TIME: *45 minutes* • DIFFICULTY: *4*

2 pounds firm fresh fish filet (snapper, bass, or swordfish)
10–12 large shrimp (preferably fresh, with head on)
18–20 Manila clams
18–20 mussels (see note, p. 101)
1 Dungeness crab, cooked, cleaned, cracked, and broken into
 pieces (see note, opposite)

---

*Jerry Dal Bozzo, *The Stinking Cookbook: The Layman's Guide to Garlic Eating, Drinking, and Stinking* (Berkely, CA: Celestial Arts, 1994).

10–12 medium to large sea scallops
1 tablespoon minced garlic
1 tablespoon minced shallots
4 ounces butter
¼ tablespoon orange zest
¼ tablespoon saffron
¼ bunch fresh basil, chopped
3 cups fish stock, canned fish broth, or clam juice (see p. 133)
1 quart marinara sauce or store-bought marinara sauce
1 cup white wine

Cut the fish filet into cubes. Remove all bones. Wash shrimp, clams, and mussels. Remove shells from shrimp (or leave them on if you prefer). Put the fish cubes, shrimp, clams, mussels, crab, and scallops in a large pot or casserole. Add fish stock and sauce, and mix. Add garlic, shallots, butter, zest, saffron, and basil, and mix again. Cook over high heat until mussels and clams open (discard unopened ones), about 10–15 minutes, covered. Serve over warm polenta (see p. 138)

NOTE:

A Web site, www.coos-bay.net/crabbingphotos.html, describes how to clean and cook crabs step by step. Alternately, you can purchase Dungeness crabmeat, already removed from the shell, at many markets. If doing the latter, use about ¾ pound of crabmeat.

75.

Salmon with Creamed Caper Sauce

The Busalacchi family has contributed a great deal to lovers of Italian food visiting or living in San Diego. In the mid-1980s, Joe Busalacchi opened the first family-owned Sicilian Restaurant in San Diego's Hillcrest area. Joe has been opening restaurants ever since, most recently a daring Italian-Asian fusion restaurant called Crudo (raw) in San Diego's Little Italy.

Meanwhile, his brother Vince has followed the family tradition and recently leapt with both feet into the restaurant business with a lovely new restaurant called Gemelli, near San Diego's Balboa Park. Vince's restaurant is a beautiful room and the food is state-of-the-art Italian. This delicious salmon dish is one of his customers' favorites.

MAKES: *4 servings* • PREPARATION TIME: *20 minutes* • DIFFICULTY: *2*

3 tablespoons butter
2 1-pound salmon filets
½ cup white wine
½ cup lemon juice, fresh or bottled

½ cup clam juice
½ cup capers
¾ cup heavy cream
Salt and pepper

Melt butter in a large skillet over medium high heat and sauté both pieces of salmon, for about two minutes, turning once. Lower heat, add white wine, lemon juice, clam juice, and capers, and simmer for about 6–7 minutes on each side or until salmon is cooked through.

Add cream for last minute of cooking, and sprinkle with salt and pepper to taste. Remove salmon from skillet, cut each filet in half, and ladle sauce over each of the four pieces.

Serve immediately.

NOTE:

Goes well with rice or a green vegetable or both.

76.

Stuffed Calamari

When we began working on our first book, *Italian Pride*, one of our early sources of information and inspiration came from Joe Anastasio and his "Italian American Web site of New York" (see p. 289). Joe was kind enough to send us this recipe passed on to him from his mother, Rose.

This recipe originated at least seventy-five years ago in Calabria, where Joe's great grandparents emigrated from. Rose remembers visiting the Fulton Fish Market in Manhattan to get the *calamari,* or squid, with her parents who would cook it up that night for dinner.

MAKES: *3–4 servings* • PREPARATION TIME: *1 hour* • DIFFICULTY: *3*

Preheat oven to 350 degrees.

3 pounds small calamari, whole
1 16-ounce can crushed tomatoes, with juice

FOR THE STUFFING:

8–10 ounces of chunk crabmeat (fresh, if possible)
1 cup Italian bread crumbs, packaged
¼ cup grated Parmesan cheese, plus more for topping
1 bud garlic, minced fine
1 tablespoon chopped fresh basil leaves
1 tablespoon chopped fresh parsley
Salt and pepper

Clean calamari lengthwise (see note below), but do not cut into pieces. Rinse sac in cold water. In a bowl, mix crabmeat, bread crumbs, cheese, garlic, basil, parsley, and salt and pepper to taste. Stuff the sac with crabmeat mixture. Place stuffed calamari into pan and cover with crushed tomatoes. Sprinkle with more grated cheese. Bake for 40 minutes.

NOTE:

To save time, ask your fishmonger for cleaned and ready-to-cook calamari. If you do it yourself, make sure you remove tentacles and everything from the eyes down, plus the bony beak at base of tentacles.

77.

Patsy's Shrimp Fra Diavolo

Pasty's has been a New York dining institution for more than sixty years, and was one of Frank Sinatra's favorite haunts. Frank especially loved seafood, and while Clams Posillipo was one of his favorites, we particularly like Patsy's very simple version of a classic Italian shrimp dish. If you want the dish to live up to its name (*Fra Diavolo* means "Brother Devil"), you should add a hefty sprinkling of red pepper flakes to the sauce, but if you like it milder, feel free to leave out the pepper and call the dish Shrimp Fra Angelico.

MAKES: *4 servings* • PREPARATION TIME: *20 minutes* • DIFFICULTY: *2*

> 1 pound capellini (angel hair) pasta.
> 3 cups (24 ounces) Fresh Tomato Sauce (see p. 77) or use Patsy's
>   own sauce, now found in many supermarkets.
> ¼ cup dry white wine (Chardonnay is best)
> ½ cup water
> 1 pound large or extra-large shrimp, peeled and deveined.

Red pepper flakes to taste (amount optional)
Salt

Bring tomato sauce to a boil over high heat and add wine, water, and cleaned shrimp. Reduce heat to medium low, add optional red pepper flakes, cover, and simmer for 7–9 minutes. Turn off heat, sprinkle lightly with salt and pour over pasta, tossing once. Serve immediately.

Vegetarian Dishes

A vegetarian can easily survive on an Italian diet. This is because so many pastas are made without meat or seafood and because Italians love to pluck the harvest of the garden and cook it before "it even knows it's been picked." Eggplant, chard, tomatoes, onions, spinach, and all kinds of egg dishes are some of the ingredients of the Italian vegetarian menu. Garbanzo beans, lentils, and cauliflower are all a part of hearty meals. Even Pasta e Fagioli, a bean and pasta dish, known throughout Italy, and Pizza Margherita are made without any meat at all. And although several of our antipasti and pasta dishes are meatless, we've also included a special vegetarian section that even has a vegan (no meat, cheese, eggs, or milk.) adaptation of lasagna sure to please even the most devoted carnivores.

78

"Chauncey Street" Frittata

East New York was once the home to many Italian families, including ours. The Moramarco family originally lived on Chauncey Street, the street made famous by the television program *The Honeymooners.*

In the old neighborhood, families used to make frittata with whatever left-overs could be found in the refrigerator. This recipe comes from the La Barbera family, close friends of our family for well over half a century, and just the smell of it evokes the most delicious memories. Adapt it in any way you choose—Ada La Barbera likes to think of it as a kind of jazz improvisation—and create wonderful memories in your kitchen as well.

MAKES: *4 servings* • PREPARATION TIME: *15 minutes* • DIFFICULTY: *2*

2 tablespoons extra virgin olive oil
Large potato, peeled and cubed
Small sweet onion, sliced
½ pound pancetta or bacon, cut into pieces (can be omitted for a
    vegetarian dish)

2 garlic cloves, minced
¾ cup green bell peppers, cubed
4 eggs
1 tablespoon milk or water
Salt
1 pound fresh spinach, cooked and well drained
2 large tomatoes, sliced
1 cup mozzarella cheese, grated
½ cup ricotta cheese
6 basil leaves, for garnish

Heat oil in a large nonstick skillet over medium-low heat and sauté the onion and pancetta or bacon (if using) for about 8 minutes (covered). Add garlic and peppers, and sauté two minutes. Scramble the eggs with the milk or water, and add to mixture. Salt lightly. Add spinach and cook for 2 more minutes, again salting lightly. Cover skillet and cook for 2–4 minutes. Add the tomatoes, mozzarella, and ricotta cheese, and let cheeses melt. Finally, garnish the dish with basil leaves.

79.

Laribe

Like many Italian families, the men in the Venzoni family were gardeners and cooks, so it wasn't at all unusual for a young boy like Dan Venzoni to grow up enjoying the art of cuisine. "I remember when they dug up potatoes they would shout *'Il nido!'* [The nest!], meaning they had found the nest where the food lived," he remembers.

This recipe is a side dish prepared throughout the northern Italian country-side. The recipe's name is derived from two Italian words: *lares,* "household goods," and *bene,* "well." So the word literally means "living well from what's around the house."

MAKES: *4 servings* • PREPARATION TIME: *50 minutes* • DIFFICULTY: *2*

    1 pound Swiss chard, stems and leaves separated, both chopped
       into 2-inch pieces
    4 medium red potatoes
    1 tablespoon extra virgin olive oil
    1 tablespoon butter

2 garlic cloves
1 small onion, chopped in pieces
Cayenne pepper

Soak chard in a sink full of water for about 5 minutes. Shake out leaves and examine closely, making sure grit and dirt is totally gone. Boil 4 medium red potatoes until a fork can be easily inserted and removed.

Heat oil and butter in a large skillet over medium-low heat and sauté garlic and onion until garlic is light brown. Do not overcook, or garlic will become bitter. Cut the stalks out of the Swiss chard and cut into small pieces and add to skillet. Toss until stalks begin to soften (about 15 minutes); then add the potatoes and sauté for another 20 minutes. Add the chard leaves and some water to the skillet to keep the mixture moist, and cook for 5–10 minutes. Season with cayenne pepper before serving.

80.

Eggplant Parmesan

This recipe comes to us from Vinny's Italian Grill and Pizzeria, a popular franchise co-owned by Vinny Vitale. Vinny now successfully operates nearly a dozen locations around Virginia and North Carolina and offers aspiring restaurateurs a chance to fulfill their dreams of opening their very own neighborhood restaurant.

Eggplant Parmesan is Vinny's house specialty. The eggplant is a member of the nightshade family, just like potatoes and tomatoes, and yes, it is technically also a fruit. Its tender, chewy slices also make it an excellent meat substitute for vegetarians.

MAKES: *4–5 servings* • PREPARATION TIME: *25 minutes* • DIFFICULTY: *2*

Preheat oven to 350 degrees.

1 large firm eggplant
Salt
2 cups of bread crumbs
Pepper
1 tablespoon chopped fresh parsley
½ cup milk

4 eggs
1 cup all-purpose flour, unbleached
Canola oil for frying
1 16-ounce jar premium tomato sauce or 2 cups Fresh Tomato
    Sauce (see p. 77)
¼ cup Parmesan cheese
Mozzarella cheese, sliced (optional)

Cut eggplant into round slices to about ½-inch thickness. Soak the eggplant in salted water or simply salt the eggplant slices to reduce bitterness. Mix bread crumbs, salt, pepper, and parsley in a bowl. In another bowl mix the milk and eggs and then whip them. Set flour in a third bowl.

Dip both sides of eggplant slices into the flour bowl. Then dip it into the milk mixture. Finally, dip it into the bread crumb mixture bowl.

Fill a frying pan with pure canola oil enough to immerse the eggplant in the oil. Heat canola oil to high temperature. Fry eggplant, once oil is hot, on both sides to a golden brown. Use a slotted spoon to transfer to paper towels to drain. When all eggplant is fried, drain excess oil from pan and place eggplant in a deep-dish ovenproof serving pan. Pour tomato sauce over the eggplant and sprinkle freshly grated Parmesan cheese on top. You can also cover with optional mozzarella cheese. Bake in oven until cheese has melted.

NOTE:

It can be served in a sandwich or on a plate along with your favorite pasta.

81.
Eggplant Meatballs

Eggplant was originally introduced to Europeans by the Arabs, who discovered it in Asia. Originally, its Latin name was *Solonum insanum*, because it was believed to cause mental illness. Eventually, cooler heads prevailed, and the eggplant has been embraced by many, although the Italians still call it *melanzane,* which roughly translates to "crazy apple."

This recipe is the perfect vegetarian alternative to meaty Italian dishes. These "meatballs" are delicious, either smothered with Fresh Tomato Sauce (see p. 77) or mixed in with fettucini and White Sauce (see p. 81).

MAKES: *4 servings* • PREPARATION TIME: *15 minutes* • DIFFICULTY: *2*

1 large eggplant
¼ tablespoon salt
Dash of pepper
½ cup chopped parsley
2 large eggs
¼ cup Parmesan cheese

½ cup Italian-seasoned bread crumbs
½ teaspoon dried basil
Pepper
Olive oil for frying

Peel eggplant and cut into 1-inch cubes. Sprinkle with salt. Bring 2 quarts of water to a boil in a medium saucepan. Add eggplant and boil over medium heat for 5 minutes. Drain. Place eggplant in clean kitchen towel and squeeze out water, being careful not to scald yourself. Put eggplant in a large bowl and mix in pepper, parsley, eggs, and cheese. Add some of the bread crumbs as needed for consistency. Set aside remaining bread crumbs in a bowl, mix with basil, and sprinkle with pepper. Form eggplant mixture into small 1-inch balls and roll balls in the bread crumb mixture. Heat olive oil in large skillet and fry until brown on all sides.

82.

Chickpea Pancakes
Panelli Fritti

Here's a fun, quick recipe for a traditional Sicilian "fast food" dish. The chickpea is another legacy from Sicily's Arabic roots. In Roman times, chickpeas were roasted as snacks. The soft, cream-colored bean is often used in salads and might be more familiar under its Spanish name, the *garbanzo* bean.

For those with wheat allergies, chickpea flour is an excellent substitute and, as you will see, can make for some tasty cakes as well.

MAKES: *about a dozen large pancakes and 4–6 servings* •
PREPARATION TIME: *10 minutes* • DIFFICULTY: *1*

3¾ cups water
1 teaspoon sea salt
3 cups sifted chickpea flour
2 teaspoons parsley, chopped fine
Pepper
Vegetable oil for frying

Put water and salt in a pot over medium heat. When water is warm, add the chickpea flour, stirring slightly to dissolve so that no lumps form. Put the saucepan over the heat, add the parsley and pepper to taste, and then mix well until it starts to thicken, coming away from sides of pan (12–15 minutes).

Use a wooden spoon to spread a small amount of the mixture out onto a platter or plate creating a ¼-inch layer. When the mixture has cooled, remove with spatula to a work surface and cut into triangular shapes. Deep fry in hot vegetable oil. Repeat steps until all the mixture has been used.

NOTE:

Serve the pancakes between 2 slices of crusty bread. If you want to add a little more Italian American flavor, spread some ricotta cheese on the sandwich.

83

Vegan Lasagna

Ross Harris, the creator of this recipe, is Italian-Irish. Sporting red hair and freckles, Ross inherited the Irish side of his family's looks, but the Italian side in his love for cooking. His grandfather and great grandfather came over to America from Rocasecca, just south of Rome.

Ross's present-day family is vegan, which means they eat neither meat nor dairy products, but that doesn't mean they can't reinvent traditional Italian dishes. "I have seen this dish overtake a traditional lasagna in popularity at family functions and end up finished off before I could get a plate," he says.

MAKES: *8 or more servings* • PREPARATION TIME: *1 hour, 15 minutes* • DIFFICULTY: *2*

1 deep dish lasagna pan, oiled with olive oil
3 14-ounce cans tomato sauce
4 tablespoons olive oil
1 bunch fresh basil, chopped
1 teaspoon dried oregano

Your favorite vegetables, sliced or chopped (Ross suggests onions,
    mushrooms, and zucchini)
3 containers of firm tofu (do not use the soft tofu)
2 boxes of noncook Semolina lasagna noodles
1 block soy mozzarella

Oil your lasagna pan; don't forget the sides. Pour the sauce into a pot and put
on medium heat as if you were making a marinara sauce for pasta, adding 2
tablespoons of the olive oil, chopped basil, and oregano to taste. Heat remaining
olive oil in large skillet, add chopped vegetables of your choice, and sauté
for 8–10 minutes; then add to the sauce.

Drain the water from the firm tofu; this is taking the place of the ricotta
cheese, so make sure it's at least as firm as that. Hand crumble the tofu into
the sauce. Simmer the sauce for about 20 minutes so that it impregnates the
tofu with flavor.

Preheat the oven to 350 degrees at 10 minutes into the sauce simmering.
When tofu is "pregnant" with saucy flavor, dish a thin layer of sauce into the
lasagna pan. Layer the lasagna noodles onto the sauce at the bottom of the pan.
Add another layer of sauce until the noodles are covered, adding a layer of soy
mozzarella to each layer. Repeat until pan is full. Pour the rest of sauce on top
to make sure the pasta is immersed in sauce and won't dry out.

Place in oven. It should take about 45 minutes for the pasta to become al
dente (cooked but firm) in the pan. Check it often to make sure it's not drying
out. Add sauce to dry areas as needed. Stick a fork in to check noodles.

When the fork pierces a noodle with ease, it's done. Grate some soy mozzarella on top with a few sprigs of basil. Place back in the oven for 5 minutes or until the cheese is melted. Let set before serving, then listen to people comment "I can't believe this has no meat or cheese!"

Pizzas and Tortas

Pizza simply means "pie" and comes in dozens of varieties. However, ask any Neapolitan, and he or she will tell you there is only one authentic kind of pizza, and that is vera pizza Napoletana (true Neapolitan pizza). Sometimes it is also known as pizza margherita, so named because it was made especially for a visit to Naples by Queen Margherita in 1889, not long after Italy had finally become a unified nation. In keeping with the rising tide of Italian patriotism, a local pizza maker, Raffaele Esposito, entered the pages of history by making a pizza with the colors of the Italian flag—red, white, and green. All he needed atop the crust was tomato sauce, cheese, and basil. Of course, even in Naples people put other things atop a crust, but when it comes to pizza, we believe that less is more. That is, a pizza overloaded with various toppings loses its distinctive flavor and often becomes a soggy glob of congested dough. Torta is a generic term for "cake" and can be either sweet or savory. The two we include in this section are of the savory variety.

84.
"Easy" Sicilian Pizza
Spiucione Siciliano

Here's a good basic pizza from Sicily, where the pan is square, the dough is thicker, and the toppings are kept to a bare minimum. This works great as an appetizer at parties or as a complete meal. If this is your first time making a pizza, try this recipe first, before moving on to thin crust.

MAKES: *6 servings* • PREPARATION TIME: *30 minutes, not including time for the dough to rise* • DIFFICULTY: *2*

FOR THE DOUGH:
3 cups all-purpose flour
1–1½ cups water
½ package dry yeast
½ teaspoon salt
Olive oil for coating

FOR THE SAUCE:
1 tablespoon olive oil
1 large sweet yellow onion, chopped
1 14-ounce can crushed tomatoes
Olive oil for drizzling
Salt and pepper
Fresh Parmesan cheese, crumbled
Bread crumbs
1½ tablespoons dried oregano
2 tablespoons fresh basil, chopped

To prepare the dough: In a medium bowl, mix flour, water, yeast, and salt to make dough. Depending on how thick you want the pizza, you can use half a packet of yeast or a quarter packet, for a thinner pizza. Knead the dough on a floured work surface for at least five minutes until it becomes soft and pliable. If necessary, add a little bit of olive oil at the end to make it a little less sticky.

Lightly coat a large bowl with olive oil. Put dough into bowl and cover loosely with a kitchen towel so that dough can rise. Let sit at room temperature for at least 30–40 minutes (or even overnight if you want a thicker pizza).

To prepare the sauce: Heat oil in a saucepan over medium heat and sauté onions until they are nice and soft. Add crushed tomatoes to make a sauce. Add a touch of olive oil and salt and pepper to taste. Turn heat to low and simmer for 20 minutes.

Preheat oven to 375–400 degrees 15 minutes before sauce is finished. When sauce is ready, spread dough out on a 3 x 9 x 12-inch baking pan. Put chunks of Parmesan cheese on top of the pizza and top with sauce. Sprinkle bread crumbs over the sauce and drizzle a little bit of olive oil over the pizza. Finally, sprinkle with oregano and basil. Put pizza in oven for 20 to 25 minutes or until golden brown.

85

The "World's Best" Pizza Margherita

Pizza is perhaps the most universally loved and quintessentially "Italian" food there is—it is also perhaps the most difficult dish to make at home.

A pizza needs to be cooked at a very high temperature; therefore, you need a special pizza baking stone to do it in a regular oven. The stone absorbs heat and transfers that hotter temperature to the pizza. You also need a pizza peal, which is a giant wooden spatula, to slide the prepared pie onto the heated stone. The process is complicated and precise, so we contacted John Arena, co-owner of Metro Pizza in Las Vegas to provide us with the details. Metro Pizza has consistently been voted one of the nation's best pizza restaurants, and they agreed to share their procedure for making Pizza Margherita.

Follow these instructions and you will have a crispy homemade pizza that will be the envy of the neighborhood. "Hand-crafted pizza is like a beautiful woman; the subtle imperfections enhance the beauty and give it character and complexity," says John Arena.

MAKES: *3 9-ounce dough balls suitable for 3 12-inch Neapolitan-style pizzas* •
PREPARATION TIME: *1 day for the dough, 1 hour for the pizza preparation* •
DIFFICULTY: *5*

Special equipment: flat baking stone for cooking pizza;
   pizza peal (see p. 5)

For the Dough:
1 cup plus 2 tablespoons of high-quality bottled water
3 teaspoons sugar
¼ ounce (or 1 package) dry yeast
4 tablespoons plus 1 tablespoon extra virgin olive oil
1 tablespoon sea salt or kosher salt
3 cups all-purpose flour

For the Toppings:
Flour for work surface
3 canned Italian whole tomatoes, peeled and well drained (see
   note 1)
Cornmeal flour for peal
Mozzarella di bufala or fresh whole milk mozzarella
1 tablespoon Italian oregano, dried
Extra virgin olive oil for drizzling

Bunch of fresh basil, finely chopped, leaving a few leaves whole
for garnish
Freshly grated Grana Padano Parmesan cheese (optional)

To prepare the dough: Place room temperature water in a large bowl. Dissolve sugar and yeast in water and wait 5 minutes. Briskly whisk in the 4 tablespoons of oil and salt to dissolve as rapidly as possible. Add flour and begin kneading dough by hand in the bowl. When dough has solidified, remove from bowl and gently knead on lightly floured surface until it is silky smooth. Divide dough into 3 equal pieces. Form each piece into a round ball. Brush with the tablespoon of olive oil and place in separate containers with tight-fitting lids. Place dough balls in refrigerator for 24 hours. The long, slow proofing process will allow the flavors to develop and will produce superior texture and aroma. You can tell when it is ready by poking it. If the indentation remains without springing back, you can go on to the next step.

To make a pizza Margherita: Place baking stone in oven and preheat to 500 degrees. Take dough ball out of refrigerator and allow it to come back to room temperature, about 30 minutes. Place dough on a well-floured surface. Using your fingertips, press a groove ½ inch from the edge of the dough. The outer edge will be the tender, puffy crown of the pizza, so never let your hands go beyond that groove as you work with the dough.

Using your fingers, press the dough to soften it, being careful not to create thin spots. When you have pressed it out to about eight inches, take the flattened disk and place it on the back of your fisted hands. Push up with your right hand, and move it forward to pull the dough across the back of your left hand, keeping your knuckles as close as possible to the ½-inch edge that you first created. Slowly continue to turn the dough in a clockwise direction until the disk expands to about 12 inches. (As you get better at this, you will be able to "spin" a pizza just like professionals using fancy aérials—but don't try this right away. Take your time.)

Place cornmeal or flour on a wooden pizza peel. Place your stretched dough on the peel (see note 2). Take the whole peeled tomatoes and crush them in a colander with a fork, draining the juice before placing on the piecrust. Repeat those steps for the remaining two dough balls.

Drain fresh mozzarella slices, and pat them dry between paper towels before placing on the pizza. Sprinkle with dried oregano, crushing the aromatic herb between your fingers as you go, and drizzle entire pie with olive oil (see variation).

Now here comes the trickiest part—transferring your beautiful pizza pie from peel to hearth. Open the oven, and using a mitt, expose the rack containing the pizza stone—that is your target. Gently shake the pizza peel to be sure the pizza will not stick. Place the peel directly over the stone, and with a quick jerk, pull out the pizza peel, leaving behind your pizza on the stone ready to cook. (If you miss your target, don't worry; at least you have two more dough balls.)

Beginners have another option—use a pizza screen or circular piece of cardboard. After carefully placing the pizza and screen or disk on the stone, let pizza settle for 3 or 4 minutes in the heated oven. Then pull out screen or disk using a fork or tongs and oven mitt, leaving the pizza behind.

Cook pizza for about 9 minutes. Never pop the bubbles and don't be afraid of dark spots on the crust. Remove the pizza from the oven, cover with fresh basil, and grate Grana Padano or Parmesan cheese (if using) onto the hot pizza. Let it sit for a minute or two. Cut, serve, and enjoy.

NOTES:

1. We highly recommend San Marzano Tomatoes for pizza sauce. If not available at specialty or grocery stores, San Marzano Tomatoes can be purchased by the case or container online at www.sanmarzanoimports.com.

2. Authors' suggestion: Oftentimes a home oven just won't get hot enough, in spite of using a pizza stone, for the crust of a pizza to cook at the same rate as the toppings. If you, too, are having this problem, try this trick: After flattening out your pie dough, transfer the naked dough to the oven to bake on the stone for a few minutes—3 or 4 at most—until it firms, but hasn't yet browned. Then, remove the partially baked dough, cool, top with the sauce and cheese, and return to the oven. This will help ensure that the crust cooks all the way through and the toppings don't burn.

VARIATION: To make a pizza with other toppings, follow directions for dough and preparation just discussed, substituting your favorite meat or vegetable toppings. However, don't put raw meat (such as sausage), mushrooms, or vegetables on the pizza; it'll make the crust soggy. Instead, heat olive oil in medium skillet and sauté sausage and other vegetables until the sausage has browned and the vegetables are soft. "Never put raw vegetables on pizza—you are not making a salad!" says John Arena.

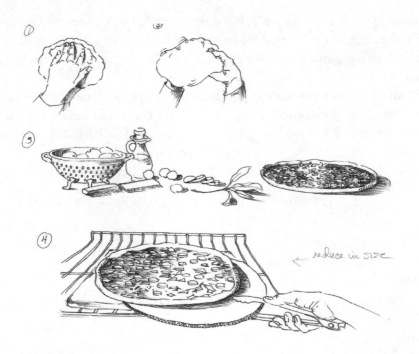

86.

Savory Country Pie
Torta Rustica

Versions of a *Torta Rustica* are made throughout Italy, as a way for families to make the most out of vegetables from their garden. A variety of cheeses are often added for additional flavoring; that is the model used at Viansa Winery, where this recipe originated.

Viansa is one of the leading producers of Italian varietals (single variety grape vines) in the United States, and its northern California vineyard is known for its lush beauty. If you visit the winery, you will discover this sumptuous pie in the deli, which always gets raves from the customers.

This dish is great warm or cold, and is perfect to serve to a crowd.

MAKES: *10 servings* • PREPARATION TIME: *1 hour, 30 minutes* • DIFFICULTY: *4*

FOR THE CRUST:
4 cups all-purpose flour
1 teaspoon salt
1 cup cold butter (2 sticks), cut into pieces
2 eggs

2 egg yolks
⅓ cup milk

For the Torta Filling:
¼ cup olive oil
2 medium leeks (white parts only), thinly sliced
1 large fennel bulb, trimmed and coarsely chopped
2 teaspoons fennel seed
2 packages (10 ounces each) frozen chopped spinach, thawed and
    squeezed dry
1 cup ricotta cheese
1 egg, beaten
¼ teaspoon salt
⅛ teaspoon pepper
⅓ cup freshly grated Parmesan cheese
⅓ cup grated mozzarella cheese
1 red bell pepper, roasted (see note, p. 27), skinned, seeded,
    deveined, and cut into thin strips
5 ounces fontina cheese, thinly sliced
1 egg yolk (to brush on crust)

To prepare the crust: Mix flour, salt, and butter in a food processor or electric mixing bowl until the mixture resembles coarse cornmeal. Beat the eggs, yolks, and milk in another bowl; then add to the processor or mixer. Mix just until the dough forms a ball. Wrap the dough tightly in plastic wrap and let rest for 30 minutes in the refrigerator.

To prepare the filling: Preheat oven to 375 degrees. Heat oil in a medium skillet over medium heat and sauté leeks, fennel, and fennel seed until limp; set aside and cool to room temperature. In a separate bowl, mix the spinach, ricotta, egg, salt, and pepper. Combine the grated Parmesan and mozzarella cheeses in a small bowl.

On a floured surface, roll out approximately three quarters of the dough into a 14- to 15-inch circle to about ⅛-inch thickness. Carefully place the dough into the springform pan, making sure the dough covers sides of pan and hangs over top at least ½ inch.

Layer the ingredients on the dough by spreading half the spinach mixture, half the red pepper strips, half the grated cheese, half the fontina slices, and half the leek and fennel mixture. Repeat the layers using the remaining ingredients.

Roll out remaining dough to the size of the top of the torta, including a ½-inch overlap, and place on top of the filled torta. Fold the dough from the bottom crust over the top and crimp the edges together, creating a lip. Use any left-over dough to make a design on the top, if desired. Lightly beat the egg yolk and brush the top of the torta.

Place on middle rack of oven. Bake for 1 hour or until golden brown. Let cool, remove from pan, and cut into wedges. Serve warm or at room temperature.

87.

Torta Tarantina

Here's a very unusual and interesting variation on pizza that comes from the city of Taranto, located in the very arch of the Italian boot. It uses baked mashed potatoes as a crust instead of pizza dough, and it's important to make sure the crust is cooked through and browned before topping with the other ingredients.. If it's still too soft, you'll end up with mashed mush instead of a pizza slice. A purist wouldn't add the porcini mushrooms, as that's not a part of the original recipe, but we think they add a lively woody flavor.

MAKES: *4 servings* • PREPARATION TIME: *50 minutes* • DIFFICULTY: *3*

> *Special equipment:* 15-inch aluminum pizza tray or flat earthenware dish

Preheat oven to 400 degrees.

> 1 ounce dried porcini mushrooms, chopped
> 2 pounds russet potatoes, peeled and quartered

⅓ cup garlic-infused extra virgin olive oil
Salt and pepper
½ pound whole milk mozzarella cheese, sliced
1 pound Roma tomatoes, peeled (see note, p. 175) seeded, and
    chopped and then drained and salted
1 teaspoon dried oregano, crumbled
Freshly ground pepper
1 tablespoon chopped fresh parsley

Soak mushrooms in warm water for 10 minutes. Boil potatoes in salted water until fork penetrates easily. Drain and put potatoes in large bowl. Mash potatoes until all lumps are gone; then add one half of the olive oil and salt and pepper to taste. Oil the pizza tray or the earthenware dish. Don't attempt to cook this directly on a pizza stone, as the potatoes won't adhere until they're baked.

Spread the potato mixture evenly over the tray, forming a pizza-like crust and bake in the oven until shell is lightly browned around the edges—at least 15 minutes or more, depending on the texture of the potatoes. *Very important:* Make sure the potato mixture is fairly crisp and solid before proceeding. If it's not, bake a bit more.

Drain water from mushrooms, blot with paper towel, and chop into small pieces. Lay the mozzarella slices evenly over the potato crust and sprinkle porcini on top. Spread tomatoes over cheese and mushrooms and sprinkle with oregano. Season with freshly ground pepper and drizzle remainder of olive oil over the torta. Bake in oven for 10 minutes or until cheese is well melted. Let cool for 5 minutes, sprinkle with chopped parsley, and serve.

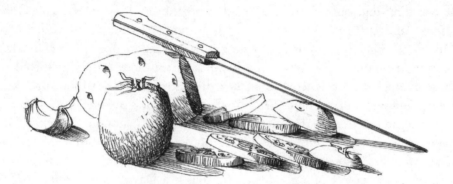

88.

Foccacia

It was amusing, but not surprising, to read the headline in the *New York Times*, January 12, 2006: "The Bread Is Famously Good But It Killed McDonald's." The story went on to note how a recently opened McDonald's restaurant in the small village of Altamura in southern Italy was forced to close because the locals rebelled against this intrusion of fast food into their long-standing culinary traditions. Initially McDonald's did well, but soon the locals began reverting to their own favorite "fast food," Altamura's famous foccacia, which costs just about the same as a MacDonald's hamburger. After less than two years in operation, McDonald's was forced to close.

Such is the power of a good foccacia that is a David to McDonald's Goliath. This recipe is not from Altamura, but it makes a damn good foccacia, although thinner than the Altamura version. You might make your local MacDonald's manager nervous if you eat it around the Golden Arches.

MAKES: *4 servings* • PREPARATION TIME: *20 minutes* • DIFFICULTY: *2*

Special equipment: flat baking stone for cooking pizza; pizza peal (see p. 5)

Preheat oven to 500 degrees.

1 pizza dough ball (see p. 225) or store bought pizza dough (see note 1)
¼ cup flour
2 tablespoons extra virgin olive oil
2 garlic cloves, thinly sliced
6 Kalamata olives, pitted and chopped
1 tablespoon rosemary, chopped
1 teaspoon fleur de sel or kosher salt

Roll pizza dough out to a 12-inch circle on a floured peal (see note 2 below), flattening edges. Sprinkle olive oil over surface and spread with a brush, so entire surface is covered. Layer garlic slices and chopped olives on top of dough and sprinkle with rosemary and fleur de sel. Slide onto pizza stone and bake until golden brown. Cool slightly, cut into pieces and serve.

NOTES:

1. Store-bought pizza dough is available at Italian markets and many specialty markets.

2. For more detailed instructions about making the dough and the use of the pizza stone see recipe #85, pp. 224–29.

Desserts

DOLCE

Italian sweets are often festive, special-occasion desserts. In the New York of the 1940s–1970s, when Italian families shared a Sunday meal, whomever the visitors might be were sure to arrive with white boxes wrapped with string and filled with delectable pastries from the local Italian bakery. In many parts of the East, this tradition remains intact, and you can get cannoli, sfugliatelle, zuppa d'Inglese, and other sweet Italian delights in many parts of the country. But you can also make some of these delights at home, and here are recipes for a festive conclusion to any meal.

89.

Ricotta Pie Nicolette

This is a cherished recipe passed down from my sister (Steve's aunt) Nicolette Moramarco. She used to make this fluffy ricotta pie in a pre-prepared pie shell that you can buy at any supermarket, but its delectable filling was always made fresh. We've "tarted" it up a bit by creating a homemade crust, which makes her recipe even more delicious. "Pizza di Ricotta" is a classic Italian dessert, and this is the best one you will ever taste.

MAKES: *8 servings* • PREPARATION TIME: *2 hours* • DIFFICULTY: *3*

> *Special equipment:* 10-inch tart pan with removable bottom;
> parchment paper or aluminum foil; dried beans or pie weights

FOR THE CRUST:
1½ cups all-purpose flour
¼ pound butter, room temperature
⅓ cup superfine granulated sugar
1 large egg yolk

1 teaspoon lemon peel, chopped fine
½ vanilla bean, split lengthwise

FOR THE FILLING:
4 large eggs
1 teaspoon vanilla extract
¼ teaspoon cinnamon
⅓ cup superfine granulated sugar
1½ pounds whole milk ricotta cheese
½ cup almonds, toasted and finely ground in processor (optional)

To prepare the crust: Mound flour on work surface. Make a well in the center and combine butter, sugar, egg yolk, and lemon peel in the well. Scrape in seeds from vanilla bean. Gradually mix flour into butter mixture, blending until coarse meal forms. Knead until just smooth. Flatten into disk and wrap in plastic. Refrigerate until firm, about an hour.

Grease and lightly flour tart pan. Roll dough out to about 12 inches and carefully transfer to prepared pan. You can slide the removable bottom of the tart pan under the rolled out dough and then lift and place in pan's rim.

Preheat oven to 325 degrees. Refrigerate crust for 15 minutes. Cut a circle of parchment or foil, line crust, and fill with dried beans or pie weights. Bake until crust is set, about 15 minutes. Remove beans and parchment. Bake crust until golden brown, about 25 minutes more. Transfer to rack and cool. Maintain oven temperature. (Crust can also be prepared 1 day ahead—just cover with plastic wrap and store at room temperature.)

To prepare the filling: Beat eggs and mix in vanilla, cinnamon, and sugar in a small bowl. Add egg mixture to ricotta in a medium bowl and mix thoroughly until well blended and relatively smooth. Pour filling into prepared crust. Bake in the 325-degree oven for about 45 minutes. During the last 10 minutes, sprinkle toasted almonds on top (if using). Cool on wire rack, remove outer rim from tart pan, and serve.

90.

Holiday Pastries with Honey or Powdered Sugar

Cartedate

Grandma Nina Moramarco made large batches of these delectable treats during both Christmas and Easter seasons. Some she would coat with honey and sprinkle with little dots of color. Others she would leave uncoated and just dust with powdered sugar. Either way, they were always a much anticipated part of the holiday seasons.

MAKES: *about 2 dozen pastries* • PREPARATION TIME: *1 hour, 15 minutes* • DIFFICULTY: *1*

Special equipment: pastry wheel

1¾ cups all-purpose flour
2½ tablespoons light olive oil
½ cup white wine
¼ teaspoon salt
Vegetable oil for frying
Honey for drizzling

Powdered sugar for dusting
Colored candy dots

Mound flour on a work surface and make a well in the center. Add olive oil, wine, and salt. Gradually incorporate liquid mixture in well into flour with a fork. Mix to make a dough and knead until smooth and elastic. Cover with a damp towel and let rest for one hour.

Roll out the pastry dough on a floured surface to a thickness of about ⅛ inch. With a pastry wheel, cut flattened dough into 1-inch-wide strips. Tie each strip into a bow, circle, or pretzel-like shape. Fry a few at a time in about an inch of hot vegetable oil (water should sizzle when dropped in) until golden brown. Drain on paper towels and cool. Drip honey over half the batch and sprinkle with colored dots. Dust other half with powdered sugar.

91.

Torta Barozzi

This is probably the most complex recipe in our book, but we couldn't resist including it. Not only is it an extra special treat, but it was contributed by the talented chef Lynne Rossetto Kasper, author of *The Splendid Table,** who discovered it in Modena.

"Cracking the code of Torta Barozzi is Modena's favorite food game," says Lynne. "For decades, local cooks have tried to unravel its mystery, without success. When a Modenese dinner party gets dull, ask about Torta Barozzi and settle back. The heat of the debate will warm you for the rest of the evening. Eugenio Gollini invented the cake in 1897 at his Pasticceria Gollini in Vignola. The cake commemorated the birthday of the Renaissance architect, Jacopo Barozzi, a native son of Vignola, who invented the spiral staircase. Today Gollini's grandsons, Carlo and Eugenio, still make Torta Barozzi at the same *pasticceria.* Its recipe is a secret, although its ingredients are stated on the cake's box. Family members have sworn never to reveal or change the formula. But Eugenio Gollini smiles severely when he tells you it is all there in plain sight."

Like a food sleuth, Lynne has painstakingly attempted to replicate the authen-

---

*Lynne Rossetto Kasper, *The Splendid Table: Recipes from Emilia-Romagna, the Heartland of Northern Italian Food* (New York: William Morrow, 1992).

tic Torta Barozzi, and she has come tantalizingly close to the original. Good luck with your own version.

MAKES: *6–8 servings* • PREPARATION TIME: *1 hour, 45 minutes cooking time* • DIFFICULTY: *5*

Special equipment: 8-inch springform pan; parchment paper

FOR THE ALMOND POWDER:
½ cup blanched almonds, toasted (see notes 1 and 2, p. 249)
2 tablespoons confectioners' sugar
3 tablespoons cocoa (not Dutch process)

FOR THE BATTER:
1½ tablespoons unsalted butter
3 tablespoons all-purpose unbleached flour
8 tablespoons unsalted butter, room temperature
½ cup plus 2 tablespoons superfine sugar
3½ tablespoons smooth peanut butter
4 large eggs, separated
5½ ounces bittersweet chocolate, melted (see note 3, p. 249) and cooled
½ ounce unsweetened chocolate, melted, and cooled
1½ tablespoons instant espresso coffee granules, dissolved in 1 tablespoon boiling water

1½ teaspoons dark rum
1 teaspoon vanilla extract

FOR THE DECORATION:
1 tablespoon cocoa (not Dutch process)
½ tablespoon confectioners' sugar

To prepare the almond powder: Combine the almonds, confectioners' sugar, and cocoa in a food processor. Process until the almonds are a fine powder (set aside).

To prepare the batter: Preheat oven to 375 degrees. Butter the bottom and sides of the springform pan with 1 tablespoon of the unsalted butter. Cut a circle of parchment paper to cover the bottom of the pan. Butter the paper as well with remaining ½ tablespoon. Coat the pan with flour and shake out any excess. Beat room temperature butter and sugar with an electric mixer at medium speed, for 8–10 minutes, or until almost white and very fluffy. When the mixture is very airy, add the peanut butter and continue beating at medium speed. Next, add the egg yolks, two at a time, and beat until smooth. Reduce the speed to medium low, and beat in the bittersweet and unsweetened melted chocolate, the dissolved coffee, the rum, and the vanilla. Fold in the almond powder with a large spatula, keeping the batter light. Whip the egg whites to stiff peaks. Lighten the chocolate batter by folding a quarter of the whites into it. Then fold in the rest, keeping the mixture light but without leaving any streaks of white.

To bake: Turn the batter into the baking pan, gently smoothing the top and bake for 30 minutes. Reduce oven temperature to 325 degrees and bake for another 15 to 20 minutes or until a steak knife inserted into center of the cake comes out relatively clean. Set pan on rack and cool. Spread a kitchen towel on a large plate and turn the cake out onto it. Peel off the parchment paper and cool completely. Finally, place a round cake plate on top of the cake and hold the two plates together as you flip them over so the torta is right-side up on the cake plate (see note 3).

NOTES:

1. *To toast almonds:* Preheat oven to 350 degrees. Spread almonds on shallow, ungreased, baking pan. Place in oven and bake for 5–10 minutes, stirring occasionally until almonds are dry, but have no color or slightly golden (your choice).

2. *To melt chocolate:* Make sure all utensils, pots, pans, and spoons are dry. Use low heat to prevent burning.

3. Torta Barozzi is moist and fudgey. Just before serving, sift the cocoa over the cake and top it with a sprinkling of confectioners' sugar. Serve at room temperature, slicing it in small wedges. The Torta Barozzi can be baked ahead, and it keeps very well if tightly wrapped in plastic wrap and stored in the refrigerator up to 3 days. It can be frozen for 2 months.

92.

Zeppole

This is a traditional fried bread, made throughout southern Italy at Christmas and on the feast of St. Josephs, and the Moramarco household in the 1940s was no exception. You could always tell the holiday season was upon us by the aroma of warm fried bread, permeating the air. My mother would pile the zeppole on a platter, sprinkled with cinnamon and powdered sugar, and the contents of the platter would sometimes mysteriously disappear long before dinner was served. In my house, we sometimes passed along a bowl of honey to dip the zeppole in. Mmmmmm.

MAKES: *about 2 dozen depending on size of dough balls* •
PREPARATION TIME: *45 minutes* • DIFFICULTY: *2*

Special equipment: large straight-sided skillet

2½ pounds all-purpose flour
1 tablespoon salt
2 cups warm water (add more if needed)

1 packet dried yeast
Canola oil for frying
Confectioners' sugar for sprinkling
Cinnamon for sprinkling

In a large bowl, put in the flour and mix in salt. In a smaller bowl, mix yeast with warm water. When it begins to foam, add to flour and mix. Add additional warm water if needed and knead until the dough is soft and pliable. Cover with a kitchen towel and set aside for about a half hour until dough rises.

Fill the skillet to about 1 inch from the top with canola oil and heat over medium-high heat. Wait until oil is very hot (a drop of water should sizzle immediately).

Rub some cold canola oil on your fingers and stretch a golf ball-sized portion of dough until it breaks off the larger piece. Drop dough balls into the hot oil, turning once until light brown all over. Drain on paper towels. Remove to large bowl and sprinkle with sugar or cinnamon or both. Serve while still warm.

93.

Grandma Phyllis's Jelly and Nut Cookies

"My mother, Phyllis Marzarella, made these cookies for Christmas and all family parties and occasions," Mary Ann Del Guercio writes to us from Manalapan, New Jersey. "Everyone always looked forward to them." Although it's called a jelly cookie, the recipe actually calls for preserves. Also, before beginning, Mary implores that you make the sign of the cross and ask Grandma to help you with these. "This is important!" she adds with emphasis. (For non-Catholics, that direction is optional of course, but don't blame us if the cookies don't turn out well.)

MAKES: *80 or 90 sliced cookies* • PREPARATION TIME: *2 hours, 30 minutes* • DIFFICULTY: *4*

Special equipment: pastry cloth or linen dish towel; 3 cookie sheets

1 cup vegetable oil
6 small eggs (or 5 large eggs)
1 cup sugar

3 teaspoons baking powder
Dash of salt
5 cups flour
1 teaspoon pure vanilla extract
Fruit preserves or jam of your choice (strawberry, raspberry, blueberry, etc.)
2 cups walnuts, chopped or crushed
Butter for greasing

For the Icing:
2 tablespoons lemon juice
½ pound confectioners' sugar

In large mixing bowl, with electic mixer, put oil, eggs, sugar, baking powder, and salt. When blended well, add flour and vanilla extract. The dough will be sticky. Refrigerate for 1–2 hours to make it easier to handle or prepare the day before.

Preheat oven to 350 degrees. Divide the dough into 6 equal pieces, about 8 ounces each. (This is where it gets tricky.) Roll dough on pastry cloth or linen dish towel, but flour it very well, or the dough will stick to it. Roll it into a long flat piece, a little shorter than your cookie sheet and about 5–6 inches wide. Spread preserves or jam (not jelly) along one side, but not close to the edge, more toward the middle, and sprinkle with chopped walnuts. Carefully fold over one long edge to the other long edge, and pinch shut with tines of a fork.

Liberally grease your cookie sheets. Transfer a long cookie to the cookie sheet, 2 long cookies to each sheet.

Bake cookies for 15–20 minutes or until the edges start to brown. Let them cool very well before icing. You can ice the next day, which is better because the jelly and cookie firm up.

To prepare icing: Slowly add the lemon juice to the sugar until it becomes the right texture for an icing. Use more juice if necessary. Ice the cookies and let icing set. Slice on an angle.

94.

Gelo di Mellone

"A kind of watermelon pudding with Oriental origins" was the only notation included with this unusual recipe from Aspra, Sicily. The recipe calls for jasmine flowers, which are edible, but not widely available as a food in America. (If you do use them, make sure they are pesticide-free.) Clifford A. Wright, author of *Cucina Paradiso: The Heavenly Food of Sicily*,* gives this explanation of its origins: "In nineteenth century and early twentieth century European scholarship, anything designated 'Oriental' meant, generally, anything east of Europe . . . Watermelon, and jasmine were introduced to Sicily by Arab traders or farmers between the ninth and thirteenth centuries." Now that we have the history aside, dive into this unusual chocolate and fruitfully divine concoction and enjoy!

MAKES: *8 servings* • PREPARATION TIME: *1 hour* • DIFFICULTY: *2*

---

*Clifford A. Wright, *Cucina Paradiso: The Heavenly Food of Sicily* (New York: Simon & Shuster, 1992).

Special equipment: foodmill or sieve

1 watermelon, about 10 pounds
3.5 ounces sugar for each quart of melon juice
2.75 ounces cornstarch for each quart of melon juice
3.5 ounces cooking chocolate (semisweet)
Jasmine flowers, for garnish (optional)

Cut the watermelon into pieces, discarding seeds and rind. Push through a food mill or sieve to get a clear juice. Measure the amount of juice and pour into a large pot over very low heat. Add correct amount of starch and sugar per quart and cook for 30 minutes, stirring constantly. As soon as mixture begins to solidify, pour it into individual glass serving dishes. Grate chocolate over the tops and add jasmine flowers (if using). Store in the refrigerator. Serve cold.

95.

Sweet "Little Ravioli" with Cherry Custard Sauce

Raviolini Dolci alla Crema di Ciliegie

"Mamma used to make ravioli on Sunday—marvelous, big ravioli stuffed with fresh ricotta and a touch of cinnamon," remembers Piero Selvaggio, owner of Valentino, in Santa Monica, California. "There was always some leftover dough and stuffing, so then she made smaller fried, sweet ravioli."

Valentino makes a stuffing with dates, amaretto, chocolate, and hazelnut. Also used is a puff pastry dough, making it more of a pastry than a ravioli, but the concept is something Mamma would approve of. This recipe takes a bit of time and skill, but the results are sure to move you closer to becoming an authentic Italian cook.

MAKES: *about 2 dozen ravioli* • PREPARATION TIME: *2 hours* • DIFFICULTY: *5*

> *Special equipment:* a 12-inch ruler, food processor with metal blade; double boiler or stainless steel bowl; ravioli or pizza cutter; nonstick baking pan

FOR THE CHERRY CUSTARD SAUCE:

2½ cups heavy cream
6 large egg yolks
½ cup granulated sugar
1 teaspoon pure vanilla extract
½ cup cherry preserves

FOR THE RAVIOLI FILLING:

½ pound pitted dates
2 tablespoons amaretto liqueur
½ cup hazelnuts, shelled
2 ounces white chocolate, chopped
3 tablespoons cream cheese
½ teaspoon ground cinnamon

FOR THE RAVIOLI:

Flour for work surface
9 ounces frozen puff pastry dough (defrosted according to instructions on package)
2 large egg whites, beaten
Confectioners' sugar for dusting

To prepare cherry custard sauce: Pour cream into a medium-size heavy-duty saucepan over medium heat and bring to a boil. In a large mixing bowl, whisk the egg yolks, sugar, and vanilla. Whisking constantly, slowly pour about 3–4 teaspoons of the warm cream into egg mixture, to temper it (see note, p. 260). Whisk in a few more tablespoons of the cream. Slowly whisk in the remaining cream and return it to the saucepan, stirring until it thickens, about 3 minutes. Do not allow it to boil. Strain the sauce through a fine sieve to remove any cooked egg particles and allow to cool. Stir in the preserves and chill for 2 hours.

To prepare the ravioli filling: Soak the dates in the amaretto until softened, about 30 minutes.

Preheat the oven to 325 degrees. Remove the shells, toast the hazelnuts on a baking sheet in the oven for 10–12 minutes, and allow to cool. Rub the nuts together in a kitchen towel to remove the skins. Finely chop and set aside.

In a food processor fitted with a metal blade, puree the dates and liquid until smooth. Transfer the mixture to a large mixing bowl.

In a double boiler, or in a stainless-steel bowl set over a pot of gently simmering water, melt the white chocolate and stir until smooth. Add it to the date mixture and stir in the cream cheese, hazelnuts, and cinnamon.

To assemble the ravioli: Preheat oven to 375 degrees. On a lightly floured work surface, unfurl the puff pastry dough to form a large rectangle. Fold pastry in half lengthwise to make seam, then open again. Working with the longest edge closest to you, use a ravioli cutter to mark off 2-inch squares in bottom half of dough without cutting through the dough. Brush the surface with egg white.

Spoon 1 rounded teaspoon of the date mixture into the center of each square. Fold the top half over bottom half, sealing the edges together. Gently press down around the outer edge of the filling to eliminate air pockets. Using ravioli cutter, cut between squares. Brush the tops with egg white.

Arrange the ravioli on a nonstick baking sheet and bake for 10 minutes. Brush again with egg white and bake another 5 minutes. Brush one more time and bake until golden brown, about 5 more minutes.

When ready to serve, spoon the custard sauce onto the individual plates, top with a ravioli, and dust with powdered sugar.

NOTE:

To temper is to prevent the egg from curdling by adding a small amount of a warm liquid, a little at a time, to the egg yolks or egg mixture, whisking constantly.

96.
Cannoli

Cannoli originated in Sicily, but are now a popular treat worldwide. Cannoli come in various sizes and with various fillings, from chocolate to fruit and nuts, but essentially they are all made from a sweetened ricotta cheese stuffed into a deep-fried hollow pastry tube.

Deep frying cannoli shells can be a tricky affair, but fortunately you can buy them at many supermarkets and Italian delis, and premade shells will work just fine. The key to good cannoli is that the cheese filling is not inserted until you are ready to serve; otherwise, the shell becomes limp.

MAKES: *12 cannoli* • PREPARATION TIME: *1 hour, 30 minutes* • DIFFICULTY: *2*

Special equipment: pastry bag (see note, p. 262)

FOR THE FILLING:
15 ounces fresh ricotta cheese
2 ounces fresh marscapone cheese
⅛ cup heavy cream

1 cup sifted confectioners' sugar
¼ teaspoon cinnamon
1 teaspoon pure vanilla extract
Green food coloring (optional)

FOR THE CANNOLI:
12 pre-made cannoli shells
1 ounce raw unsalted pistachio nuts, crushed (optional)

To prepare filling: Mix the ricotta and marscapone cheeses, cream, sugar, cinnamon and vanilla in a bowl with an eggbeater or mixer on low until smooth. Add a few drops of food coloring (if using), for a festive color. Refrigerate for at least an hour to let the mixture settle.

To assemble cannoli: Place the mixture in a pastry bag and fill the cannoli shell from both ends. Dip ends in crushed pistachios (if using). Sprinkle with more confectioners' sugar and serve immediately or within the hour.

NOTE:

If you do not have a pastry bag, cut the tip off a plastic bag, fill it, and squeeze the mixture into both ends of the cannoli shell or spoon fill.

VARIATIONS: You may add chocolate chips, sprinkles, or candied fruits (along with a tiny bit of lemon zest) to the cannoli mixture.

97.
Garlic Ice Cream

Yes, you read the title of this recipe correctly. When we started collecting recipes for this book, we contacted our friends at The Stinking Rose in San Francisco's North Beach for a couple of good garlic recipes, and boy did they deliver. In addition to the Cioppino recipe (p. 194), they gave us this one, which is one of the most unconventional uses of garlic we can think of—in ice cream! Owner Jerry Dal Bozzo says that people looking at the dessert menu are skeptical—until they taste it. Surprise your family or guests with this one-of-a-kind dessert. And you don't even need an ice cream maker to prepare it!

MAKES: *6–8 servings* • PREPARATION TIME: *20 minutes to make; then a few hours to freeze* • DIFFICULTY: *1*

3 cups whole milk
¼ teaspoon freshly chopped garlic
1 vanilla bean, split in half lengthwise
1 cup heavy cream

1½ cups granulated sugar
9 egg yolks

Put milk, garlic, and entire vanilla bean in a saucepan. Bring to a boil and re-move from heat. In a mixing bowl, blend cream, sugar, and egg yolks. Remove hull of vanilla bean and strain the scalded milk mixture into the cream mix-ture in the bowl, stirring constantly. Return the combined mixture to the same pan and stir constantly over moderate heat until mixture coats the back of a spoon, about 10–15 minutes. Cool in an ice bath; then freeze until firm.

98.
Struffoli

As sweet as this honey-dripped dessert can be, it can also be a source of contention. In the DellaVecchia family, Papa Mario likes to make struffoli into a hardened wreath, as described in the following recipe, but Mama Theresa likes to add the honey at the end, so it is hot and fresh. "Family arguments would be peppered with accusations of incorrect struffoli making," son Frank remembers.

This recipe makes for a large dinner-sized plate of struffoli—plenty to get a family through a large meal. Try making it both ways, and decide for yourself which is superior.

MAKES: *4 or more servings* • PREPARATION TIME: *1 hour, 45 minutes* •
DIFFICULTY: *3*

> *Special equipment:* deep fryer or 12- to 14-inch skillet with 3-inch
>   sides; deep-fry thermometer

3 eggs
5 tablespoons sugar
¼ teaspoon salt
1½ tablespoons olive oil
2 cups all-purpose flour
Flour for work surface
Vegetable oil for deep frying
1 cup honey
Blanch roasted almonds (optional) (see note, p. 249)

In a bowl, whisk the eggs, 1 tablespoon of the sugar, salt, and olive oil. Stir flour into egg mixture. If the dough is too tacky, stir in a very tiny amount of flour. Work mixture with your hands into a soft dough. Place dough in bowl, cover with plastic wrap, and let settle for about an hour.

Divide dough into 4 or 5 pieces. On floured surface, roll each piece into a rope about the width of your index finger and 12 inches long. Cut ropes into ¾-inch pieces. Toss the pieces with enough flour to dust them lightly, and shake off excess flour.

In a deep fryer or skillet heat vegetable oil to 375 degrees. When hot, fry the struffoli a few handfuls at a time until puffed up and golden color. Transfer with a slotted spoon to paper towels to drain.

In a large saucepan, combine honey and remaining half cup of sugar. Add blanched roasted almonds (if using) and heat honey until sugar is dissolved. Remove from heat, add the fried balls, and stir gently with a wooden spoon.

Transfer to plate and place the struffoli pieces in a circle around the edge, forming a wreath. When struffoli cools and hardens, it is ready to eat.

NOTE:

If you make this for a Christmas meal, you can put a poinsettia flower or some pine cones in the center to create a festive display.

99

Almond Biscotti

Italians have been making these long, curved, hard cookies for ages. They love to dip them in coffee, wine, or any other handy beverage. Biscotti are literally "twice-baked" biscuits and keep for a long while in an airtight container. They're great to have around the house when an unexpected craving arises.

Lately, the Italian love for biscotti has invaded America. These are ubiquitous at coffee shops throughout the land. And they're not cheap—at about $1.50 a piece, a biscotti habit can quickly become expensive. This recipe will cost you one tenth of that and keep you supplied for several weeks.

MAKES: *30 biscotti* • PREPARATION TIME: *1 hour* • DIFFICULTY: *4*

Special equipment: parchment paper or nonstick baking liner

2 cups all-purpose flour
¾ cup superfine (Baker's) sugar (see note, p. 270)
1 teaspoon baking powder

⅛ teaspoon salt
3 large eggs
1 teaspoon pure vanilla extract
½ teaspoon almond extract
1 cup blanched almonds, toasted and chopped
   into small pieces
Flour for work surface

Preheat oven to 300 degrees. Line a baking sheet with parchment paper or nonstick baking liner. In a large bowl, mix flour, sugar, baking powder, and salt until well blended. Whisk egg and vanilla and almond extracts in a small bowl, and gradually add the egg mixture to the flour mixture, beating on slow speed with an electric mixer.

After 2 minutes, add almonds and continue beating until dough forms. Remove dough from bowl to a floured surface and divide ball into two logs each about 2 x 10 inches. Place both logs side by side several inches apart on prepared baking sheet and bake for about 35 minutes until logs are fairly firm, but not hard. Remove from oven and cool for about 10 minutes. When logs are cool enough to touch, transfer to a cutting board, and using a serrated knife, cut diagonally into 1½-inch slices. Return slices to baking sheet and bake 10 minutes on one side; then turn and bake an additional 10 minutes on the other side until biscotti are quite firm and brown. Let cool and store in airtight container.

NOTE:

Baker's sugar can be ordered online at www.bakerssugar.com, or you can try to find both Baker's and Domino superfine in your grocery store.

VARIATIONS: Additional flavorings like anise extract, orange zest, or cinnamon can be added to the dough, and walnuts, hazelnuts, pecans, or pine nuts can be substituted for the almonds.

100.

Tiramisu

Tiramisu means "pick me up," and it's intended to be an upbeat and light dessert to finish off a fabulous meal. The recipe for this version comes from Dominic's Restaurant on the Hill in St. Louis, Missouri, one of the most venerable and highly regarded restaurants in the area. We asked Dominic about the sweet marsala wine and the sambuca liqueur in his version, and he attributed them to his Sicilian origins but insisted that we be careful not to use too much. "It's a dessert, not an after-dinner drink," he said. In any case, his tiramisu is intoxicating and we recommend it highly.

MAKES: *8 servings* • PREPARATION TIME: *1 hour plus time for chilling* • DIFFICULTY: *3*

> *Special equipment:* glass casserole or baking dish to hold
>   20 ladyfingers
>
> 6 large eggs, separated
> 1 cup Baker's sugar (see note, p. 270)

12 ounces mascarpone cheese
½ ounce sambuca liqueur
2½ cups espresso coffee
½ cup sweet marsala wine
40 ladyfingers
3 ounces semisweet chocolate,
    grated
Cocoa powder, unsweetened,
    for dusting

Raspberries (optional)
Strawberries (optional)
Blueberries (optional)

Beat the egg yolks, sugar, and mascarpone together in a large bowl with an electric mixer until the texture is creamy. Add the sambuca.

In a separate bowl, whip egg whites until soft peaks form, then fold them into the mascarpone mixture. Combine the espresso and marsala in another large bowl.

Place a 9 x 12-inch glass casserole or baking dish large enough to hold 20 ladyfingers on your work surface. Place your espresso mixture next to dish. Quickly dip ladyfingers into the espresso mixture, and place moistened ladyfingers side by side in the dish. (They will soften on their own.)

Repeat with remaining ladyfingers, laying them in the opposite direction of the bottom layer and spread the remaining marscarpone mixture over the top layer. Sprinkle with grated chocolate and dust the entire top of the cake with cocoa. Chill for four hours.

Garnish with berries (if using) before serving.

NOTE:

You can substitute amaretto or other liqueur for a different flavor.

And to wash it all down...

101.

Limoncello

Our friend Nico Calavita recently returned from Italy and was struck by the popularity of an after-dinner drink called Limoncello. Essentially, it's a hard alcohol distilled with lemon and sugar. Everywhere he went, he would see people quaffing down glasses of the stuff in the waning hours after a long dinner.

While a version of Limoncello can be bought here in the United States, it's much more fun to be your own "bootlegger" and make it at home. Some areas of the country may not have grain alcohol, so vodka can be substituted.

And since we've provided your palate with 100 flavorful dishes, we offer Nico's recipe as number 101. *Buona fortuna!*

MAKES: *about 1 pint Limoncello* • PREPARATION TIME: *1 week (!), then 2 hours* • DIFFICULTY: *2*

Special equipment: 1-quart glass jar with tight lid

4 large lemons, peeled
1 pint pure grain alcohol (see note below) or vodka
1 pound sugar
1 pint water

Peel the lemons (save peeled lemons for other use) and add lemon peels to the alcohol. Store the mixture in a tightly closed jar and in a dark place for a week. On the seventh or eighth day, bring a pint of water to a boil. Add the sugar until it is dissolved and the mixture is syrupy. Strain the lemon peels from the lemon-infused alcohol mixture and add mixture to the sugared water. Stir well and store in freezer.

NOTE:

Only certain states allow pure grain alcohol to be sold, but the Web site www.beerliquors.com carries Everclear, a 190 proof or 95 percent pure alcohol.

Putting Together Whole Meals

Here are just a few examples of entire menus you can plan using the recipes in Deliciously Italian. Wine pairings are courtesy of our guest sommelier, Aldo Blasi of Ristorante Milano in San Francisco and Luca Vannini of Zigzagando Wines. Naturally, we don't expect you'll serve all these wines with each course, but these suggestions might make it easier for you to find wines that will go well with the meals. If you can't find the specific vineyard, try to find something similar. The grape the wine is made from or the type of wine is listed first; the vineyard follows the dash. For example, if you can't find a Sauvignon Blanc from Casa Zuliani to go with the Spaghettini all' Agli e Olio, you might want to substitute a Sauvignon Blanc from another Italian vineyard. (If you want to "Americanize" the menu a bit, try a Sauvignon Blanc from California, New York, or Washington State.)

Quick and Easy Complete Italian Dinners

Tomatoes with Basil, Olive oil,
and Mozzarella, #1
Almond Biscotti, #99

Spaghettini all' Agli e Olio, #35
Veal Piccata, #69

Main Course Wines:
Sauvignon Blanc—Casa Zuliani

Sangiovese "Rocca Ventosa"
—Cantina Tollo

Dessert Wines:
Moscato—Gianni Gagliardo

Recioto—Buglioni

Blood Orange and Onion Salad, #15
Braciole Sicilian Style, #65

Rigatoni with Ricotta, #33
Store-bought Gelato

Main Course Wines:
Barbera D'Alba—Gianni Gagliardo

Pinot Nero—Terre di Gioia

Dessert Wine:
Gewürztraminer—Cortaccia

Operatic Spring Greens with
    Gorgonzala, Walnuts, Currants,
    and Three-Cheese Dressing, #16
Garlic Ice Cream, #97

Risotto Milanese, #49
 Biba Caggiano's Broiled
    Cornish Game Hens, #55

MAIN COURSE WINES:

Barbera "Bricco Cichetta"
—Pietro Rinaldi

Montepulciano "Valle D'Oro"
—Cantina Tollo

Weekend Dinners with Friends

Federico and Stephen's "Instant"
Antipasto Misto, #2
Sweet "Little Ravioli" with
Cherry Custard Sauce, #95

Italian Wedding Soup, #19
Grilled Lamb Chops with
Sautéed Vegetables, #67

MAIN COURSE WINES:

Sfursat "Ca Rizzieri"—Rainoldi

Vino Nobile Montepulciano
Riserva—Fanetti

DESSERT WINES:

Dolcetto D'Alba—Gianni Gagliardo

Muller Thurgau—Cortaccia

Bruschetta or Crostini, #6
Fettucini with Arugula and Goat
Cheese, #41

Prosciutto-Wrapped Shrimp, #9
Osso Buco, #63
Tiramisu, #100

MAIN COURSE WINES:
Vino Nobile Montepulciano—Fanetti   Inferno Riserva—Rainoldi

DESSERT WINE:
Gewürtztraminer—Cortaccia

Parmesan Chips, #13
Spinach and Apple Salad, #17
Penne alla Giulietta, #34

Caponatina alla Siciliana with
    Crisp Italian Bread, #5
Chicken Broccolatini, #54

MAIN COURSE WINES:
Inferno Riserva—Rainoldi

Barbaresco "Rabaja"—
    Cascina Luisin

DESSERT DRINK:
Limoncello, #101

Very Classic Italian

Roasted Peppers with Cheese, #8
Spaghetti with Mama's Sunday
    Sauce, #31

Red Garbanzo Broth, #23
Gelo dé Mellone, #94

MAIN COURSE WINES:

Vino Nobile Montepulciano —Fanetti

Cabernet, Sangiovese, "Sala martano"—Montellori

Vegetarian

Rice Croquettes, #7
Vegan Lasagna, #83

Stracciatella, #22
Italian Pride Salad, #18

MAIN COURSE WINES:

Dolcetto D'Alba—Gianni Gagliardo

Chianti DOCG—Montellori

An Italian Super Bowl Sunday

Federico and Stephen's "Instant" Antipasto Misto, #2
Moretti Beer

Parmesan Chips, #13
The "World's Best" Pizza Margherita, #85

A Feast of the Seven Fishes (Christmas Eve)

Fried Smelt, #12
Patsy's Shrimp Fra Diavolo, #77
Salmon with Creamed Caper Sauce, #75

Cioppino #74
Calamari stuffed with Crabmeat, #76
Holiday Pastries with Honey or Powdered Sugar, #90

MAIN COURSE WINES:
Ischia Bianco—Pietratorcia

Sauvignon Bianco—Cortaccia

DESSERT WINE:
Moscato—Gianni Gagliardo

Participating Restaurants

Contained within this book are recipes from some of America's best Italian chefs and restaurants. If you live in, or are visiting, one of the areas below, you can't go wrong by visiting one of these fine establishments. We suggest you call first to confirm hours, find location, and make reservations.

Albona
(Capuzi Garbi, #14)
545 Francisco St.
San Francisco, CA 94133
(415) 441-1040

Apertivo Restaurant
(Prosciutto-Wrapped Shrimp, #9)
3926 30th St.
San Diego, CA 92104
(619) 297-7799

Arrivederci Restaurant
(Fettucini with Arugula and Goat Cheese,
    #41)
3845 4th Ave.
San Diego, CA 92103-3113
(619) 299-6282
www.arrivedercirestorante.com

Aurora Trattoria
(Osso Buco, #63)
1025 Prospect St. #250
La Jolla, CA 92037
(858) 551-8554

Biba Restaurant
(Broiled Cornish Game Hens, #55)
2801 Capitol Avenue
Sacramento, CA 95816
(916) 455-2422

Buon Appetito
(Polenta, Forrester's Style, #52)
1609 India St.
San Diego, CA 92101
(619) 238-9880

Ca' Brea Restaurant
(Pan-Roasted Lamb Loin with Black
    Olives, #66)
346 South La Brea Ave.
Los Angeles, CA 90036
(323) 938-2863
www.cabrearestaurant.com

Café on the Green Restaurant
(Pasta and Bean Soup, #24)
100 Aunt Hack Rd.
Danbury, CT 06811
(203) 791-0369
www.cafeonthegreenrestaurant.com

Campagnola Restaurant
Veal alla "Ecco," #68
1382 1st Ave.
New York, NY 10021
(212) 861-1102

Carbonara Trattoria
(Stracciatella, #22)
111 Avenida Del Mar # B.
San Clemente, CA 92672
(949) 366-1040
www.carbonara.com

Charlie Gitto's on the Hill
(Braciole, Sicilian-Style, #65)
5226 Shaw Avenue
St. Louis, MO 63110
(314) 772-8898
www.charliegittos.com

Cicolella in Fiera
(Troccoli, Foggia-Style, #42, Grilled Lamb
    Chops with Sautéed Vegetables, #67)
Viale Fortore 155
71100 Foggia (FG)
Italy 0881632166
www.hotelcicolella.it

Dominic's on the Hill
(Tiramisu, #100)
5101 Wilson Ave.
St. Louis, MO 63110
(314) 771-1632
www.dominicsrestaurant.com

Frank Papa's Ristorante
(Veal alla "Diana," #70)
2241 South Brentwood Blvd.
Saint Louis, MO 63144
(314) 961-3344

Gemelli Italian Grill
(Salmon with Creamed Caper Sauce, #75)
495 Laurel St.
San Diego, CA 92101
(619) 234-1050

Gramercy Tavern
(Roasted Tomatoes with Polenta, #53)
42 East 20th St.
New York, NY 10003
(212) 477-0777

Grifone Restaurant
(Tagliatelle Porcini, #47)
244 East 46th St.
New York, NY 10017
(212) 490-7275

Hosteria Mazzei
(Sautéed Sea Scallops with Eggplant and
    Porcini Mushrooms, #74)
25 S. Regent St.
Port Chester, NY 10573
(914) 939-2727

Il Cortile Restaurant
(Risotto Frutti di Mare, #50)
125 Mulberry St.
New York, NY 10013
(212) 226-6060

Il Melograno
(Cavatelli with White Beans and Mussels,
    #37)
Contrada Torricella No. 3
Monopoli, 70043
Italy
39-0806-909030
1-866-LUXE-411
www.melograno.com

La Rivera Restaurant
(Crabmeat Ravioli, #46)
506 Shores Dr.
Metairie, LA 70006
(504) 888-6238

La Scala
(Artichoke Hearts with Crabmeat, #11)
1012 Eastern Ave.
Baltimore, MD 21202
(410) 783-9209

Lusardi's Restaurant
(Seared Sea Scallops on a Potato and
   Chive Cake with White Truffles, #72)
1494 2nd Ave.
New York, NY 10021
(212) 249-2020

Magnifico Restaurant
(Chicken Scarpiella, #58)
200 9th Ave.
New York, NY 10011
(212) 633-8033

Metro Pizza
(The "World's Best" Pizza Margherita,
   #85)
4178 East Koval Ln.
Las Vegas, NV 89109
(702) 736-1955
www.metropizza.com

Monica's
(Stuffed Zucchini, #4)
67 Prince St.
Boston, MA 02113
(617) 720-5472
www.monicasonline.com

Patsy's Italian Restaurant
(Patsy's Shrimp FraDiavolo, #77)
236 West 56th St.
New York, NY 10019
(212) 247-3491
www.patsys.com

**Po Pazzo (Spaghetti with Mama's
   "Sunday Sauce," #31)**
1917 India St.
San Diego, CA 92101
(619) 238-1917

Primavera Restaurant
(Minestrone, #21)
830 East Oakland Park Blvd.
Oakland Park, FL 33334
954-564-6363
www.restaurantprimavera.com

Ristorante ai Due Ghiottoni
(Risotto ai Due Ghiottoni, #51)
Via Putignani 11
Bari, Italy
80-523-2248

Ristorante Milano
(Rice with Radicchio and Taleggio
Cheese, #48)
1448 Pacific Ave.
San Francisco, CA 94109
(415) 673-2961

San Marco Ristorante
(Raspberry Chicken, #56)
658 Motor Parkway
Hauppauge, NY 11788
(800) 510-0088
www.sanmarcoristorante.com

Sotto Sopra
(Foie Gras Gnocchi, #43)
405 North Charles St.
Baltimore, MD 21201
(410) 625-0534
www.sottosoprainc.com

The Stinking Rose
(Cioppino, #74, and Garlic Ice Cream,
#97)
325 Columbus Ave.
San Francisco, CA 94133
(415) 781-7673
www.thestinkingrose.com

Trattoria Contadina
(Roasted Peppers with Cheese, #8)
1800 Mason St.
San Francisco, CA 91433
(415) 982-5728
www.trattoriacontadina.com

Trattoria La Siciliana
(Penne alla Giulietta, #34)
2993 College Ave.
Berkeley, CA 94704
(510) 704-1474

Valentino, Los Angeles
(Parmesan Chips, #13, Fusilli with
    Olives, Peas, and Pecorino, #32,
    "Sweet Ravioli" with Cherry Custard
    Sauce, #95)
3115 Pico Blvd.
Santa Monica, CA 90405
(310) 829-4313
www.welovewine.com

Venticello
(Spinach and Apple Salad, #17)
1257 Taylor St.
San Francisco, CA 94108
(415) 922-2545
www.venticello.com

Viansa Winery and Italian Marketplace
(Savory Country Pie, #86)
25200 Arnold Dr.
Sonoma, CA 95476
(800) 995-4740
www.viansa.com

Vinny's at Night
(Chicken Broccolatini, #54)
76 Broadway
Somerville, MA 02145
(617) 628-1921

Vinny's Italian Grill and Pizzeria
(Eggplant Parmesan, #80)
11105 Leavells Rd.
Fredericksburg, VA. 22407
540-710-5517
www.vinnysitaliangrill.com

zazu
(Cotecchino with Lentils, Bacon, and
    Truffle Oil, #71)
3535 Guerneville Rd.
Santa Rosa, CA 95436
(707) 477-4288

And thanks to:
Lynne Rossetto Kasper
(Torta Barozzi, #91)
splendidtable.publicradio.org/

APPENDIX C

Participating Families

In addition to the Moramarcos, the following families have graciously opened their hearts (and their cookbooks) and offered up some of their traditional Italian family favorites for you to enjoy.

The Anastasio Family, *Calabria*
Stuffed Calamari, #76
www.italian-american.com/main.htm

The Calavita Family, *Brindisi*
Limoncello, #101

The Chironna Family, *Altamura*
Eggplant Meatballs, #81, Orecchiette
  with Potatoes and Arugula, #36

The Clerico Family, *Piedmont*
Piedmont Autumn Soup, #20

The DellaVecchia Family, *Nusco*
Hunter's Chicken, #57, Struffoli, #98

The Di Fiore Family, *Bagheria, Sicily*
Caponatina alla Siciliana, #5, Gelo di
  Mellone, #94, Pasta with Sardines,
  Anchovies, and Fennel Sauce, #39

The Giametta Family, *Sicily*
Pasta with Zucchini, #40

The Harris Family, *Rocasecca*
Vegan Lasagna, #83

The Maggiore Family, *Maschito, Potenza*
Italian Skillet, #60

The Marinese Family, *Abruzzi*
Stuffed Artichokes, #3

The Marzarella Family, *Sicily*
Grandma Phyllis's Jelly and Nut Cookies, #93

The Rinaldi Family, *Gemona di Friuli*
Pork Shoulder in Milk, #62

The Tinelli Family, *Calabria*
Fried Smelt, #12
www.feastofthesevenfishes.com

The Venzoni Family, *Fonzaso, Comunanza*
Laribe, #79, Grandma's Four-Cheese Ravioli, #45

The Vitale Family, *Palermo, Sicily*
Chickpea Pancakes, #82, "Easy" Sicilian Pizza, #84

APPENDIX D

Acknowledgments

The following recipes were reprinted courtesy of the publishers:

Cioppino, and Garlic Ice Cream from *The Stinking Cookbook: The Layman's Guide to Eating, Drinking and Stinking* by Jerry Dal Bozzo, © 1994 by Jerry Dal Bozzo adapted and reprinted by permission.

Pan Roasted Lamb Loin with Black Olives from *Italy Anywhere: Living an Italian Culinary Life Wherever You Call Home* by Lori De Mori, Jean-Louis De Mori, and Antonio Tommasi, © 2000, by Lori De Mori and Antonio Tommasi. Used by Permission of Viking Pengiun, a division of Penguin Group (USA), Inc.

Red Garbanzo Broth from *The Art Of Cooking: The First Modern Cookery Book Composed by the Eminent Maestro Martino of Como* © 2005, and used by permission of University of California Press.

Torta Barozzi from *The Splendid Table* by Lynn Rosetto Kasper, © 1992, by Lynn Rosetto Kasper and reprinted by permission of Harper Collins Publishers, William Morrow.

Rock Game Cornish Hens from *Northern Italian Cooking* by Biba Caggiano, © 1987, by HP Books, The Berkley Publishing Group, a division of Penguin Group (USA) Inc.

Braciole, Sicilian-Style, Tiramisu from *The Hill: Its History, Its Recipes* by Eleanore Berra Marfisi, © 2003, and used by permission of G. Bradley Publishing.

Special Thanks to Our Fabulous Tasters and Testers:

Arturo and Penelope Andrade, Jack Black, Kim Buresh, Andrew Burgess, Nico and Kitty Calavita, Teresa Davis, Francis DellaVecchia, Sabrina Drill, Erin Ellescas, Melodee Fernandez, Dean Fisher, Ron Frank, Jean Gilbert, S. A. Griffin, Sage Guyton, Josh Haden, Tanya Haden, Dana Harris, Elizabeth Herndon, Billy and Ronna Joseph, Ivan Kasimoff, David Koff, John Lambertson, Claire Lloyd, Lisa Lopez, David Markowitz, Ethan Markowitz, Harrison Maxwell, Clarissa Moramarco, Dave Moore, Lee Nichols, Michael Perrick, Lorraine Perrotta, Michael Plüss, James Rowe, Deena Rubinson, Felicia Rusnak, Erin Shull, Deborah Smaller, Doug Stewart, Jennifer Teft, Evan Urkofsky, Dan Venzon, Gary Viggers, Ryan Vincent, Kim Welch, Erika Westbrook, Jessica White, Michael "Vince" Wintz, Rob Zabrecky

For more information, visit www.italianpride.com—The home of all things great Italian!

Index